SHAKESPEARE'S SONNETS

NOTES

including
- *Life and Background of the Poet*
- *Introduction to the Sonnets*
- *An Overview of the Sonnets*
- *Critical Essay*
- *Review Questions and Essay Topics*
- *Selected Bibliography*

by
Carl Senna, M.F.A.
The Providence Journal

Cliffs Notes

INCORPORATED

LINCOLN, NEBRASKA 68501

Acquisitions Editor

Greg Tubach

Project Editor

Kathleen M. Cox

Copy Editor

Kathleen Dobie

Library of Congress No.:99-69722
ISBN 0-7645-8617-3
© Copyright 2000
by
Cliffs Notes, Inc.
All Rights Reserved
Printed in U.S.A.

2000 Printing

Cliffs Notes, Inc.   Lincoln, Nebraska

CONTENTS

•

CRITICAL ESSAY 107

REVIEW QUESTIONS AND ESSAY TOPICS.....110

SELECTED BIBLIOGRAPHY 111

First Lines to Sonnets

6

SHAKESPEARE'S SONNETS

Notes

LIFE AND BACKGROUND OF THE POET

Born in 1564, William Shakespeare was the eldest son of John and Mary Shakespeare. Shakespeare's father was a landowner who raised sheep, and a well respected guild member in Stratford-Upon-Avon. The prestige and respect Mr. Shakespeare earned in his lifetime afforded him and his descendants the honor of being granted a coat of arms in 1596, a promotion from commoner to gentry status.

In 1582, William Shakespeare's name appears on a marriage certificate at Trinity Church along with his wife Anne Hathaway. They had three children, Susanna , and twins Hamnet and Judith. Hamnet died in 1596. Shakespeare apparently left for London around 1586. Although it cannot be known with certainty, his first plays—*Titus Andronicus, Henry VI,* and *The Comedy of Errors*—were performed in London sometime between 1588 and 1594. His mythological love poem "Venus and Adonis" was published in 1593, followed the next year by "The Rape of Lucrece," both dedicated to the Earl of Southampton. Theaters in London were closed due to the plague, leaving Shakespeare time to write poetry. It's believed he wrote most of the sonnets during this period, as well. Shakespeare's greatest writing period ranged from 1599 to 1608, when he wrote such masterpieces as *Twelfth Night, Hamlet, Othello, King Lear,* and *Macbeth.* All told, Shakespeare is known to have written thirty seven plays, two narrative poems, and the sonnets from 1588 through 1613.

On March 25, 1616, William Shakespeare revised his last will and testament. He died on April 23 of the same year, and his body was buried within the chancel and before the altar of Trinity Church in Stratford. A rather wry inscription is chiseled into his tombstone:

Good friend for Jesus' sake forbear,
To dig the dust enclosed here!
Blest be the man that spares these stones,
And curst be he who moves my bones.

The last direct descendant of William Shakespeare was his granddaughter, Elizabeth Hall, who died in 1670.

INTRODUCTION TO THE SONNETS

A sonnet is a 14-line poem that rhymes in a particular pattern. In Shakespeare's sonnets, the rhyme pattern is *abab cdcd efef gg*, with the final couplet used to summarize the previous 12 lines or present a surprise ending. The rhythmic pattern of the sonnets is the iambic pentameter. An *iamb* is a metrical foot consisting of one stressed syllable and one unstressed syllable—as in dah-DUM, dah-DUM dah-DUM dah-DUM dah-DUM. Shakespeare uses five of these in each line, which makes it a pentameter. The sonnet is a difficult art form for the poet because of its restrictions on length and meter.

Although the entirety of Shakespeare's sonnets were not formally published until 1609 (and even then, they were published without the author's knowledge), an allusion to their existence appeared eleven years earlier, in Francis Meres' *Palladis Tamia* (1598), in which Meres commented that Shakespeare's "sugred Sonnets" were circulating privately among the poet's friends. Approximately a year later, William Jaggard's miscellany, *The Passionate Pilgrim*, appeared, containing twenty poems, five of which are known to be Shakespeare's—two of the Dark Lady sonnets (Sonnets 138 and 144) and three poems included in the play *Love's Labour's Lost*. Apparently these five poems were printed in Jaggard's miscellany (a collection of writings on various subjects) without Shakespeare's authorization.

Without question, Shakespeare was the most popular playwright of his day, and his dramatic influence is still evident today, but the sonnet form, which was so very popular in Shakespeare's era, quickly lost its appeal. Even before Shakespeare's death in

1616 the sonnet was no longer fashionable, and for two hundred years after his death, there was little interest in either Shakespeare's sonnets, or in the sonnet form itself.

The text of Shakespeare's sonnets generally considered to be definitive is that of the 1609 edition, which was published by Thomas Thorpe, a publisher having less than a professional reputation. Thorpe's edition, titled *Shake-speare's Sonnets: Never Before Imprinted,* is referred to today as the "Quarto," and is the basis for all modern texts of the sonnets.

The Quarto would have lapsed into obscurity for the remainder of the seventeenth century had it not been for the publication of a second edition of Shakespeare's sonnets, brought out by John Benson in 1640. A pirated edition of the sonnets, Benson's version was *not* a carefully edited, duplicate copy of the Quarto. Because Benson took several liberties with Shakespeare's text, his volume has been of interest chiefly as the beginning of a long campaign to sanitize Shakespeare. Among other things, Benson rearranged the sonnets into so-called "poems"—groups varying from one to five sonnets in length and to which he added descriptive and unusually inept titles. Still worse, he changed Shakespeare's pronouns: "He's" became "she's" in some sonnets addressed to the young man so as to make the poet speak lovingly to a woman—not to a man.

Benson also interspersed Shakespeare's sonnets with poems written by other people, as well as with other non-sonnet poems written by Shakespeare. This led to much of the subsequent confusion about Shakespeare's order of preference for his sonnets, which appear to tell the story, first, of his adulation of a young man and, later, of his adoration of his "dark lady."

The belief that the first 126 sonnets are addressed to a man and that the rest are addressed to a woman has become the prevailing contemporary view. In addition, a majority of modern critics remain sufficiently satisfied with Thorpe's 1609 ordering of those sonnets addressed to the young man, but most of them have serious reservations about the second group addressed to the woman.

Another controversy surrounding the sonnets is the dedication at the beginning of Thorpe's 1609 edition. Addressed to "Mr. W. H.," the dedication has led to a series of conjectures as to the identity of this person. The two leading candidates are Henry Wriothesley, third Earl of Southampton, and William Herbert, third Earl of Pembroke.

Because Shakespeare dedicated his long poem "Venus and Adonis" to Southampton, and because the young earl loved poetry and drama and may well have sought out Shakespeare and offered himself as the poet's patron, many critics consider Southampton to be "Mr. W. H."

The other contender for the object of the dedication is William Herbert, Earl of Pembroke. Shakespeare dedicated the First Folio of his works, published in 1623, to Pembroke and Pembroke's brother Philip. Pembroke was wealthy, notorious for his sexual exploits but averse to marriage, and a patron of literary men. Critics who believe that Mary Fitton, one of Queen Elizabeth's maids of honor, was the Dark Lady of Sonnets 12–54, are particularly convinced that Pembroke is "Mr. W. H.," for Pembroke had an affair with Fitton, who bore him a child out of wedlock; this extramarital affair is considered to parallel too closely the sexual relationship in the sonnets to be mere coincidence.

In addition to their date of composition, their correct ordering, and the object of the dedication, the other controversial issue surrounding the sonnets is the question of whether or not they are autobiographical. While contemporary criticism remains interested in the question of whether or not the sonnets are autobiographical, the sonnets, taken either wholly or individually, are first and foremost a work of literature, to be read and discussed both for their poetic quality and their narrative tale. Their appeal rests not so much in the fact that they may shed some light on Shakespeare's life, nor even that they were written by him; rather, their greatness lies in the richness and the range of subjects found in them.

AN OVERVIEW OF THE SONNETS

Although Shakespeare's sonnets can be divided into different sections numerous ways, the most apparent division involves Sonnets 1–126, in which the poet strikes up a relationship with a young man, and Sonnets 127–154, which are concerned with the poet's relationship with a woman, variously referred to as the Dark Lady, or as his mistress.

In the first large division, Sonnets 1–126, the poet addresses an alluring young man with whom he has struck up a relationship. In Sonnets 1–17, he tries to convince the handsome young man to marry and beget children so that the youth's incredible beauty will not die when the youth dies. Starting in Sonnet 18, when the youth appears to reject this argument for procreation, the poet glories in the young man's beauty and takes consolation in the fact that his sonnets will preserve the youth's beauty, much like the youth's children would.

By Sonnet 26, perhaps becoming more attached to the young man than he originally intended, the poet feels isolated and alone when the youth is absent. He cannot sleep. Emotionally exhausted, he becomes frustrated by what he sees as the youth's inadequate response to his affection. The estrangement between the poet and the young man continues at least through Sonnet 58 and is marked by the poet's fluctuating emotions for the youth: One moment he is completely dependent on the youth's affections, the next moment he angrily lashes out because his love for the young man is unrequited.

Despondent over the youth's treatment of him, desperately the poet views with pain and sorrow the ultimate corrosion of time, especially in relation to the young man's beauty. He seeks answers to the question of how time can be defeated and youth and beauty preserved. Philosophizing about time preoccupies the poet, who tells the young man that time and immortality cannot be conquered; however, the youth ignores the poet and seeks other friendships, including one with the poet's mistress (Sonnets 40–42) and another with a rival poet (Sonnets 79–87). Expectedly, the relationship between the youth and this new poet greatly upsets the sonnets' poet, who lashes out at the young man and then retreats into despondency, in part because he feels his poetry is lackluster and cannot compete with the new forms of poetry being written about the youth. Again, the poet fluctuates between confidence in his poetic abilities and resignation about losing the youth's friendship.

Philosophically examining what love for another person entails, the poet urges his friend not to postpone his desertion of the poet—if that is what the youth is ultimately planning. Break off the relationship now, begs the poet, who is prepared to accept whatever fate holds. Ironically, the more the youth rejects the poet, the greater is the poet's affection for and devotion to him. No matter how vicious the young man is to the poet, the poet does not—emotionally can not—sever the relationship. He masochistically accepts the youth's physical and emotional absence.

Finally, after enduring what he feels is much emotional abuse by the youth, the poet stops begging for his friend's affection. But then, almost unbelievably, the poet begins to think that his new-found silence toward the youth is the reason for the youth's treating him as poorly as he does. The poet blames himself for any wrong the young man has done him and apologizes for his own treatment of his friend. This first major division of sonnets ends with the poet pitiably lamenting his own role in the dissolution of his relationship with the youth.

The second, shorter grouping of Sonnets 127–154 involves the poet's sexual relationship with the Dark Lady, a married woman with whom he becomes infatuated. Similar to his friendship with the young man, this relationship fluctuates between feelings of love, hate, jealousy, and contempt. Also similar is the poet's unhealthy dependency on the woman's affections. When, after the poet and the woman begin their affair, she accepts additional lovers, at first the poet is outraged. However, as he did with the youth, the poet ultimately blames himself for the Dark Lady's abandoning him. The sonnets end with the poet admitting that he is a slave to his passion for the woman and can do nothing to curb his lust. Shakespeare turns the traditional idea of a romantic sonnet on its head in this series, however, as his Dark Lady is not an alluring beauty and does not exhibit the perfection that lovers typically ascribe to their beloved.

Quotes are taken from the Pelican Shakespeare edition of *The Sonnets*, published by Penguin books.

CRITICAL COMMENTARIES

SONNET 1

Shakespeare begins his sonnets by introducing four of his most important themes—immortality, time, procreation, and selfishness—which are interrelated in this first sonnet both thematically and through the use of images associated with business or commerce.

The sonnet's first four lines relate all of these important themes. Individually, each of these four lines addresses a separate issue. Line 1 concerns procreation, especially in the phrase "we desire increase"; line 2 hints at immortality in the phrase "might never die"; line 3 presents the theme of time's unceasing progress; and line 4 combines all three concerns: A "tender heir" represents immortality for parents, who will grow old and die. According to the sonnet's poet, procreating ensures that our names will be carried on by our children. If we do not have children, however, our names will die when we do.

But, the scenario the poet creates in these four lines apparently has been rejected by the young man, whom the poet addresses as "thou," in lines 5–12. Interested only in his own selfish desires, the youth is the embodiment of narcissism, a destructively excessive love of oneself. The poet makes clear that the youth's self-love is unhealthy, not only for himself but for the entire world. Because the young man does not share himself with the world by having a child to carry on his beauty, he creates "a famine where abundance lies" and cruelly hurts himself. The "bud" in line 11 recalls the "rose" from line 2: The rose as an image of perfection underscores the immaturity of the young man, who is only a bud, still imperfect because he has not fully bloomed.

The final couplet—the last two lines—reinforces the injustice of the youth's not sharing his beauty with the world. The "famine" that he creates for himself is furthered in the phrase "To eat the world's due," as though the youth has the responsibility and the world has the right to expect the young man to father a child. Throughout the sonnets, Shakespeare draws his imagery from everyday life in the world around him. In Sonnet 1, he writes of love in terms of commercial usury, the practice of charging exorbitant interest on money lent. For example, in the first line, which reads, "From fairest creatures we desire increase," "increase" means not only nature's gain through procreation but also commercial profit, an idea linked to another trade term, "contracted," in line 5. In line 12, by using the now-antiquated term "niggarding," which means hoarding, the poet implies that the youth, instead of marrying a woman and having children, is selfishly wasting his love all for himself.

(Here and in the following sections, unfamiliar words and phrases are explained.)

- **churl**   rude person.
- **plenitude**   plenty.

SONNET 2

Sonnet 2 continues the argument and plea from Sonnet 1, this time through the imagery of military, winter, and commerce. Time again is the great enemy, besieging the youth's brow, digging trenches—wrinkles—in his face, and ravaging his good looks. Beauty is conceived of as a treasure that decays unless, through love, its natural increase—marrying and having children—is made possible.

The poet attempts to scare the young man into marrying and having children by showing him his future. When the youth is forty years old, he will be nothing but a "tottered weed" (meaning tattered garment), "of small worth held" because he will be alone and childless. The only thing the young man will have to look back on is his self-absorbed "lusty days," empty because he created nothing—namely, no children. This barrenness of old age is symbolized in the sonnet's last line, "And see thy blood warm when thou feel'st it cold," and contrasts to the previous sonnet's spring imagery.

The poet's argument that the young man is actually hurting himself by not procreating is present in this sonnet as it was in the preceding one. This time, however, the youth's narcissism is both physical and emotional. The poet predicts that by the time the youth turns forty years old, he will have "deep-sunken eyes," and the shame he will feel for not having children will be an "all-eating" emotion, which recalls the phrases "Feed'st thy light's flame" and "this glutton be" from Sonnet 1.

Again drawing on business imagery, the poet acknowledges that all he seeks is for the young man to have a child, who would immortalize the youth's beauty. The poet does not call the act of love "increase," as he did in Sonnet 1, but "use," meaning investment, the opposite of "niggarding" from Sonnet 1. In line 8, he speaks of "thriftless praise," or unprofitable praise—the term "thrift" during Shakespeare's lifetime had various meanings, including profit and increase, which also recalls Sonnet 1.

"Proud livery" in line 3, here meaning well-tailored clothing, contrasts to "tottered weed" as the clothes of a nobleman's servant contrast to the rags of a beggar; the phrase also refers to the youth's outward beauty, which time devours. To refrain from marriage makes the youth guilty of narcissism and of cruelty to future generations. A "thriftless" victim of time, he is symbolized by "winters" rather than by years.

SONNET 3

Drawing on farming imagery, the poet focuses entirely on the young man's future, with both positive and negative outcomes. However, the starting point for these possible futures is "Now," when the youth should "form another," that is, father a child.

The sonnet begins with the image of a mirror—"Look in thy glass"—and is repeated in the phrase "Thou art thy mother's glass." Continuity between past, present, and future is established when the poet refers to the young man's mother, who sees her own image in her son and what she was like during her youth, "the lovely April of her prime," a phrase that recalls the images of spring in Sonnet 1. Likewise, the young man can experience a satisfying old age, a "golden time," through his own children.

The negative scenario, in which the young man does *not* procreate, is symbolized in the poet's many references to death. In lines 7 and 8, the poet questions how the young man can be so selfish that he would jeopardize his own immortality. The reference to death in line 14 stylistically mirrors the death imagery in the final couplets of the preceding sonnets, including the phrases "the grave and thee" in Sonnet 1 and "thou feel'st it cold" in Sonnet 2.

- **uneared**   untilled.
- **tillage**   cultivated land.

SONNET 4

The themes of narcissism and usury (meant here as a form of *use*) are most developed in this sonnet, with its references to wills and testaments. The terms "unthrifty," "legacy," "bequest," and "free" (which in line 4 means *to be generous*), imply that nature's generosity should be matched by those who benefit from it. The poet, who calls the youth a "beauteous niggard," or a miser of his good looks, claims that his young friend abuses the many gifts of beauty nature has given him and thus is a "profitless usurer," a business term that recalls the three previous sonnets.

Sonnet 4 summarizes all that the poet has been saying thus far. In a series of questions and statements, the poet lectures about the wise use of nature, which liberally lends its gifts to those who are equally generous in perpetuating nature by having children. But the youth's hoarding contrasts to nature's bountifulness. Lines 7 and 8 express this contrast in terms of usury: "Profitless usurer, why dost thou use / So great a sum of sums, yet canst not live?" The term *use* here means both invest and use up. Similarly, "live" means both to gain immortality and to make a living.

The inevitable conclusion is that if the youth does not properly use his beauty, he will die childless and doom himself to oblivion, but if he fathers a child, he will be remembered. The final couplet presents these contrasting possibilities. Line 13 uses familiar death imagery to express the negative result of dying childless: "Thy un-used beauty must be tombed with thee." However, line 14 suggests that should the young man use his beauty to have a child, an "ex-ecutor to be," his beauty will be enhanced because he will have used it as nature intended.

SONNET 5

Sonnet 5 compares nature's four seasons with the stages of the young man's life. Although the seasons are cyclical, his life is lin-ear, and hours become tyrants that oppress him because he cannot escape time's grasp. Time might "frame / The lovely gaze where every eye doth dwell," meaning that everyone notices the youth's beauty, but time's "never-resting" progress ensures that this beauty will eventually fade.

In an extended metaphor, the poet argues that because flowers provide perfume to console people during the winter, it is natural for the youth to have a child to console him during his old age. Without perfume from summer's flowers, people would not re-member previous summers during the long, hard winters; child-less, the young man will grow old alone and have nothing to remind him of his younger days.

Winter, an image of old age, is regarded with horror: "Sap checked with frost and lusty leaves quite gone, / Beauty o'ersnowed and bareness everywhere." The "lusty leaves" imagery recalls the "lusty days" from Sonnet 2 and reemphasizes the barrenness of the youth's old age, in which he will look back longingly on his younger days but have nothing to remember them by. However, in the final couplet, the poet evokes a comforting tone, suggesting that immortality is attainable for the young man, just as it is for summer's flowers when they are transformed into perfume, if only the young man would father a child.

- **distill(ed)** reduced to the essence.

SONNET 6

Sonnet 6 continues the winter imagery from the previous sonnet and furthers the procreation theme. Winter, symbolizing old age, and summer, symbolizing youth, are diametrically opposed.

The poet begs the young man not to die childless— "ere thou be distill'd"—without first making "sweet some vial." Here, "distill'd" recalls the summer flowers from Sonnet 5; "vial," referring to the bottle in which perfume is kept, is an image for a woman whom the young man will sexually love, but "vial" can also refer to the child of that sexual union. Ten children, the poet declares, will generate ten times the image of their father and ten times the happiness of only one child.

The poet strongly condemns the young man's narcissism in this sonnet by linking it with death. "Self-killed" refers both to the youth's hoarding his beauty by not passing it on to a child, and to his inevitably dying alone if he continues his narcissistic behavior. The poet argues that procreation ensures life after death; losing your identity in death does not necessarily mean the loss of life so long as you have procreated. Lines 5 and 6 make this concept clear: "That use is not forbidden usury / Which happies those that pay the willing loan." Once you recognize the wealth of beauty by loving another person, you must use this knowledge of love if it is to increase and not decay.

Sonnet 6 is notable for the ingenious multiplying of conceits and especially for the concluding pun on a legal will in the final couplet: "Be not self-willed, for thou art much too fair / To be death's conquest and make worms thine heir." Here, as earlier in the sonnet, the poet juxtaposes the themes of narcissism and death. "Self-willed" echoes line 4's "self-killed," and the worms that destroy the young man's dead body will be his only heirs should he die without begetting a child.

SONNET 7

Sonnet 7 compares human life to the passage of the sun ("gracious light") from sunrise to sunset. The sun's rising in the morning symbolizes the young man's youthful years: Just as we watch the "sacred majesty" of the ever-higher sun, so too does the poet view the youth. The sun's highest point in the sky resembles "strong youth in his middle age." However, after the sun reaches it apex, its only direction is down. This downward movement represents "feeble age" in the youth, and what is worse than mere physical appearance is that the people who looked in awe at the youth's beauty will "look another way" when he has become old. In death, he will not be remembered.

As usual, the poet argues that the only way for the youth to ensure that he is remembered after he dies is to have a child, making it clear that this child should be a son. Two possible reasons why the poet wants the young man to have a son and not a daughter are that, first, a son would carry on the youth's last name, whereas traditionally a daughter would assume the last name of her husband, and second, the word "son" is a play on the word "sun"—it is not coincidental that in this sonnet, which incorporates the image of the sun, the poet makes clear for the first time that the young man's child should be a son.

• **car** cart.

SONNET 8

In this sonnet, the poet compares a single musical note to the young man and a chord made up of many notes to a family. The marriage of sounds in a chord symbolizes the union of father, mother, and child.

The first twelve lines elaborate a comparison between music and the youth, who, should he marry and have a child, would then be the very embodiment of harmony. But music, "the true concord of well-tuned sounds," scolds him because he remains single—a single note, not a chord. By refusing to marry, the youth destroys the harmony that he should make as part of an ensemble, a family. Just as the strings of a lute when struck simultaneously produce one sound, which is actually made up of many sounds, so the family is a unit comprised of single members who function best—and most naturally—when working in tandem with one another.

• **concord**   harmony, agreement.

SONNET 9

The poet imagines that the young man objects to the bliss of marriage on the grounds that he might die young anyway or that he might die and leave a bereaved widow and an orphaned child. To these arguments, the poet replies that should the young man marry, have a child, and then die, at least his widow will be consoled by the child whom the young man fathered; in this way, his image will not be destroyed with his death. Furthermore, by not marrying, the young man makes the whole world his widow.

Shakespeare continues the business imagery so prevalent in the previous sonnets. The concept of love is not entirely distinguished from commercial wealth, for Shakespeare relates those who traffic in love to the world at large. When an unthrifty person makes ill use of his inherited wealth, only those among whom he squanders it benefit. The paradox lies in the fact that the hoarding of love's beauty is the surest way of squandering it: Such consuming self-love unnaturally turns life inward, a waste felt by all.

• **makeless**   mateless.

SONNET 10

Sonnet 10 repeats and extends the argument of Sonnet 9, with the added suggestion that the youth really loves no one. Clearly, the poet does not seriously believe the young man to be incapable of affection, for then there would be no point in the poet's trying to maintain a relationship with him. However, underneath the mock-serious tone is the poet's suggestion that the youth's self-love wastes himself. Narcissism means infatuation with one's own appearance, but the youth's absorption with his own image is really an attachment to nobody. He therefore loses the power of returning the creative force of love in a relationship. The poet considers the youth's unwillingness to marry a form of homicide against his potential progeny, which he suggested in Sonnet 9: "The world will wail thee like a makeless wife;/ The world will be thy widow, and still weep . . ." And in Sonnet 10, the poet writes, "For thou art so possessed with murdrous hate/ that 'gainst thyself thou stick'st not to conspire." Here, Sonnet 10 creates the image of marriage as a house with a roof falling in decay that the youth should seek to repair, but the poet uses the house imagery less to indicate marriage than to suggest the youth's beauty would reside in his offspring: "Make thee another self for love of me,/ That beauty still may live in thine or thee."

SONNET 11

The poet now argues that the young man needs to have a child in order to maintain a balance in nature, for as the youth grows old and wanes, his child's "fresh blood" will act as a balance to his own old age. The young man is irresponsible not to have a child, for if others acted as he does, within one generation the entire human population would die out. The young man's actions are not only irresponsible; they are also unnatural. Nature, according to the poet, intended people who are able to have children to have them. Those people who refuse to have children are unnatural and upset nature's balance.

Encouraging the youth to reproduce, the poet draws an analogy between procreation and writing poetry. The images of Sonnet 11 suggest that procreation and posterity reflect art and craftsmanship: "She carved thee for her seal, and meant thereby / Thou shouldst print more, not let that copy die." The young man, should he die childless, effectively kills any lasting image of himself through his children.

SONNET 12

Sonnet 12 again speaks of the sterility of bachelorhood and recommends marriage and children as a means of immortality. Additionally, the sonnet gathers the themes of Sonnets 5, 6, and 7 in a restatement of the idea of using procreation to defeat time. Sonnet 12 establishes a parallel way of measuring the passage of time, the passage of nature, and the passage of youth through life—decay. Lines 1 and 2 focus on day becoming night (the passage of time); lines 3 and 4 link nature to humankind, for the poet first evokes a flower's wilting stage (the passage of nature). Then, in line 4, the poet juxtaposes this image with black hair naturally aging and turning gray (the passage of youth)—an allusion perhaps meant to frighten the young man about turning old without having created a child. The poet then discusses the progression of the seasons, from "summer's green" to "the bier with white and bristly beard," which is an image of snow and winter. By stressing these different ways to measure time's decay, the poet hopes that the young man will finally realize that time stops for no one; the only way the young man will ensure the survival of his beauty is through offspring. This final point, that having children is the single means of gaining immortality, is most strongly stated in the sonnet's concluding couplet: "And nothing 'gainst Time's scythe can make defense / Save breed, to brave him when he takes thee hence." In these lines, "Time's scythe," a traditional image of death, is unstoppable "save breed," meaning except by having children. The fast pace of time, or the loss of it, remains a major theme in the sonnets.

Sonnet 12 is notable for its musical quality, thanks largely to the effective use of alliteration and attractive vowel runs, which are of unusual merit. This sonnet, along with Sonnet 15, which is also notable for its musical quality, is almost always included in anthologies of lyric poetry. Note the striking concluding lines and how they convey the sense of sorrow and poignancy at the thought that youth and beauty must be cut down by time's scythe. The contrast of "brave day" with "hideous night" is particularly good. And, as one critic has pointed out, the sonnets beginning with "When" are especially noteworthy because the structure of such sonnets is periodic (consisting of a series of repeated stages), making for tightness of organization, logical progression, and avoidance of a tacked-on couplet, while admirably evoking seasonal change.

- **erst**   formerly.

SONNET 13

Sonnet 13 furthers Sonnet 12's theme of death by again stating that death will forever vanquish the young man's beauty if he dies without leaving a child. Some significance may lie in the fact that the poet refers to the youth as "you" in Sonnet 13 for the first time. "Thou" expresses respectful homage in Elizabethan parlance, but "you" expresses intimate affection. In any case, Sonnet 13 begins with the heartfelt wish, "O, that you were yourself," and the warning, ". . . but, love, you are / No longer yours than you yourself here live." This second line reminds the youth that at death, he will cease to possess himself because he has no offspring to perpetuate his name and his beauty.

The poet's proposal to his friend in Sonnet 13 contains ambiguities. Indeed, the young man may choose either to have a son or to remain only an image of himself when he looks in a mirror. Substance (a son) or form (the youth's image in a mirror) is the only choice presented. The young man seems so completely immersed in his own personality that his entire being is in doubt. Already the poet hints of deceit, which now the youth unwittingly uses against himself and later deliberately uses against the poet. By refusing to marry, the youth cheats himself of happiness and denies his continuation in a child.

The concluding couplet presents a new argument on the poet's part in persuading the young man to marry and procreate. Earlier in the sonnets (Sonnets 3 and 8), the poet invoked the young man's mother as a persuasive tool. Here, the poet asks why the youth would deny a son the pleasure of having the young man as his father, just as the young man found happiness in being the son of *his* father. And perhaps even more important, the poet questions why the young man would deny himself the rapture of fatherhood when he has plainly observed the joy of his own father's being a parent to him.

SONNET 14

Sonnet 13 depends on an intimate relationship between the poet and the young man that is symbolized in the use of the more affectionate "you"; Sonnet 14 discards—at least temporarily—this intimate "you" and focuses on the poet's own stake in the relationship between the two men. In fact, this sonnet is more about the poet—the "I"—than about the young man. Ironically, the poet appears to be as infatuated with the young man as he claims the young man is infatuated with his own reflection in a mirror.

Sonnet 14 contains one dominant image, that of the young man's eyes as stars, from which the poet attains his knowledge. Stylistically, this sonnet is a good example of a typical Shakespearean sonnet: The first eight lines establish an argument, and then line 9 turns this argument upside down with its first word, "But." The concluding couplet, lines 13 and 14, declares some outcome or effect of the young man's behavior. Typically, this concluding image is of death, as in Sonnet 14's "Thy end is truth's and beauty's doom and date." In other words, should the young man die without fathering a son, not only will he suffer from the lack of an heir, but the world, too, will suffer from the youth's selfishness.

SONNET 15

In Sonnet 15's first eight lines, the poet surveys how objects mutate—decay—over time: ". . . every thing that grows / Holds in perfection but a little moment." In other words, life is transitory and ever-changing. Even the youth's beauty will fade over time, but because the poet knows that this metamorphosis is inevitable, he gains an even stronger appreciation of the young man's beautiful appearance in the present time—at least in the present time within the sonnet. Ironically, then, the youth's beauty is both transitory and permanent—transitory because all things in nature mutate and decay over time, and permanent because the inevitable aging process, which the poet is wholly aware of as inevitable, intensifies the young man's present beauty: Generally, the more momentary an object lasts, the more vibrant and intense is its short life span.

Sonnet 15 also introduces another major theme that will be more greatly developed in later sonnets: the power of the poet's verse to memorialize forever the young man's beauty. "I ingraft you new," the poet says at the end of the sonnet, by which the poet means that, however steady is the charge of decay, his verses about the young man will keep the youth's beauty always fresh, always new; the sonnets immortalize this beauty. Ironically, the poet's sonnets serve the same purpose as a son whom the poet wants the young man to father: They perpetuate the youth's beauty just as a son would. In fact, the sonnets are even more immortal than a son. The sonnets continue to be read even today, whereas the young man's progeny may have completely died out.

• **vaunt**   boast.

SONNET 16

Sonnet 16 continues the arguments for the youth to marry and at the same time now disparages the poet's own poetic labors, for the poet concedes that children will ensure the young man immortality more surely than will his verses because neither verse nor painting can provide a true reproduction of the "inward worth" or the "outward fair" of youth.

Although the poet has tried to immortalize the youth's beauty in his sonnets, the youth's sexual power is, as line 4 states, endowed "With means more blessed than my barren rhyme." The poet concedes that his poetry ("painted counterfeit") is "barren" because it is a mere replica of the young man's beauty and not the real thing itself, whereas a child ("the lines of life") will keep the young man's beauty alive and youthful in a form more substantial than art can create.

SONNET 17

In the earlier sonnets, the poet's main concern was to persuade the youth to marry and reproduce his beauty in the creation of a child. That purpose changes here in Sonnet 17, in which the poet fears that his praise will be remembered merely as a "poet's rage" that falsely gave the youth more beauty than the youth actually possessed, thus expressing an insecurity about his poetic creations that began in the preceding sonnet.

This disparaging tone concerning the sonnets is most evident in line 3, in which the poet characterizes his poetry as a "tomb." Such death imagery is appropriate given the frequent incorporation of time, death, and decay images throughout the first seventeen sonnets. Ironically, the poet, who has been so concerned about the young man's leaving behind a legacy at death to remind others of his priceless beauty, is now worried about *his own* future reputation. Will his poems be ridiculed by readers who disbelieve the poet's laudatory praise of the young man's beauty? Not, says the poet, if the youth has a child by which people can then compare the poet's descriptions of the youth's beauty to the beauty of the youth's child—now asking the youth to have a child in order to confirm the poet's worthiness.

The sonnet's concluding couplet links sexual procreation and versification as parallel activities: "But were some child of yours alive that time, / You should live twice—in it and in my rime." The poet's task is an endless struggle against time, whose destructive purpose can only be frustrated by the creation of fresh beauty or art, which holds life suspended.

SONNET 18

One of the best known of Shakespeare's sonnets, Sonnet 18 is memorable for the skillful and varied presentation of subject matter, in which the poet's feelings reach a level of rapture unseen in the previous sonnets. The poet here abandons his quest for the youth to have a child, and instead glories in the youth's beauty.

Initially, the poet poses a question—"Shall I compare thee to a summer's day?"—and then reflects on it, remarking that the youth's beauty far surpasses summer's delights. The imagery is the very essence of simplicity: "wind" and "buds." In the fourth line, legal terminology—"summer's lease"—is introduced in contrast to the commonplace images in the first three lines. Note also the poet's use of extremes in the phrases "more lovely," "all too short," and "too hot"; these phrases emphasize the young man's beauty.

Although lines 9 through 12 are marked by a more expansive tone and deeper feeling, the poet returns to the simplicity of the opening images. As one expects in Shakespeare's sonnets, the proposition that the poet sets up in the first eight lines—that all nature is subject to imperfection—is now contrasted in these next four lines beginning with "But." Although beauty naturally declines at some point—"And every fair from fair sometime declines"—the youth's beauty will not; his unchanging appearance is atypical of nature's steady progression. Even death is impotent against the youth's beauty. Note the ambiguity in the phrase "eternal lines": Are these "lines" the poet's verses or the youth's hoped-for children? Or are they simply wrinkles meant to represent the process of aging? Whatever the answer, the poet is jubilant in this sonnet because nothing threatens the young man's beautiful appearance.

Then follows the concluding couplet: "So long as men can breathe, or eyes can see, / So long lives this, and this gives life to thee." The poet is describing not what the youth *is* but what he *will be* ages hence, as captured in the poet's eternal verse—or again, in a hoped-for child. Whatever one may feel about the sentiment expressed in the sonnet and especially in these last two lines, one cannot help but notice an abrupt change in the poet's own estimate of his poetic writing. Following the poet's disparaging reference to his "pupil pen" and "barren rhyme" in Sonnet 16, it comes as a surprise in Sonnet 18 to find him boasting that his poetry will be eternal.

SONNET 19

In Sonnet 19, the poet addresses Time and, using vivid animal imagery, comments on Time's normal effects on nature. The poet then commands Time not to age the young man and ends by boldly asserting that the poet's own creative talent will make the youth permanently young and beautiful. However uninspired the sonnet as a whole might seem, the imagery of animals is particularly vivid.

The sonnet's first seven lines address the ravages of nature that "Devouring Time" can wreak. Then, in line 8, the poet inserts the counter-statement, one line earlier than usual: "But I forbid thee one most heinous crime." The poet wants time to leave the young man's beauty untouched. Note that the word "lines" in line 10 unquestionably means wrinkles; in the previous sonnet, "lines" had at least three possible meanings.

Although the poet begs time not to ravish the young man's beauty, to leave it "untainted" as an example of perfection ("beauty's pattern") upon which all can gaze, the concluding couplet, especially line 13's beginning "Yet," underscores the poet's insecurity of what he asks for. However, nature's threatening the youth's beauty does not matter, for the poet confidently asserts that the youth will gain immortality as the subject of the sonnets. Because poetry, according to the poet, is eternal, it only stands to reason that *his* poetry about the young man will ensure the youth's immortality. The youth as the physical subject of the sonnets will age and eventually die, but in the sonnets themselves he will remain young and beautiful.

SONNET 20

In this crucial, sensual sonnet, the young man becomes the "master-mistress" of the poet's passion. The young man's double nature and character, however, present a problem of description: Although to the poet he possesses a woman's gentleness and charm, the youth bears the genitalia ("one thing") of a man, and despite having a woman's physical attractiveness, the young man has none of a woman's fickle and flirtatious character—a condescending view of women, if not flat out misogynistic.

The youth's double sexuality, as portrayed by the poet, accentuates the youth's challenge for the poet. As a man with the beauty of a woman, the youth is designed to be partnered with women but attracts men as well, being unsurpassed in looks and more faithful than any woman.

Sonnet 20 is the first sonnet not concerned in one way or another with the defeat of time or with the young man's fathering a child. Rather, the poet's interest is in discovering the nature of their relationship. Yet even as the poet acknowledges an erotic attraction to the youth, he does not entertain the possibility of a physical consummation of his love.

Of all the sonnets, Sonnet 20 stirs the most critical controversy, particularly among those critics who read the sonnets as autobiography. But the issue here is not what *could* have happened, but what the poet's feelings are. Ambiguity characterizes his feelings but not his language. The poet does not want to possess the youth physically. But the sonnet is the first one to evoke bawdiness. The poet "fell a-doting" and waxes in a dreamlike repine of his creation until, in the last line, the dreamer wakes to the youth's true sexual reality: "Mine be thy love, and thy love's use their treasure." We are assured then that the relation of poet to youth is based on love rather than sex; according to some critics, even if the possibility existed that the poet *could* have a sexual relationship with the young man, he doesn't show that he would be tempted. Other critics, of course, disagree with this interpretation.

SONNET 21

Having explored the nature of his and the young man's relationship in the previous sonnet, the poet now returns to his theme of immortality. Not only does he grant the youth immortality through his verse, but because the poet's enduring love is repeatedly stressed as well, the poet himself gains a kind of immortality. Disclaiming kinship with the inconstant poetry of "painted beauty," he announces his only standard in the plea: "O let me, true in love, but truly write."

In Sonnet 21, the poet notes for the first time the presence of a rival poet; whether this is the same rival of later sonnets is unclear. Whereas in Sonnet 20 the youth's portrait was drawn from nature, in Sonnet 21 his appearance is concealed by cosmetics. Regretfully, the youth prefers inflated rhetoric and flattery to the poet's restraint, plainness, and sincerity. The criticism of the rival poet—"that Muse"—stems from the poet's view that too much hyperbole and artificiality indicate insincerity and false sentiment. Lack of sincerity, by extension, also is considered here an aspect of bad art. The poet criticizes the rival in a double sense, using the method of pretended understatement as a rhetorical device that contrasts the rival's superficial poetic style. Thus the phrase "fair / As any mother's child" sufficiently praises the youth, or anyone for that matter. But to say in the concluding couplet, "Let them say more than like of hearsay well; / I will not praise that purpose not to sell," reveals that the poet is himself engaging in a kind of excessive, elaborate, and affected eulogy. At any rate, the point of Sonnet 21 is that the poet speaks truth and the rival poet hyperbolizes.

- **rondure**   sphere.

SONNET 22

Until now, the poet's feelings have soared to the level of rapture; in Sonnet 22, he suggests—perhaps deluding himself—that his affections are being returned by the youth. He declares that the youth's beauty "Is but the seemly raiment of my heart, / Which in thy breast doth live, as thine in me." To reconcile himself to his physical decline caused by aging, the poet argues that so long as he holds the youth's affection, he and the youth are one and the same; he can defy time and his own mortality because he measures his physical decline by how the young man ages. So long as the youth remains young, so will the poet.

The image of the poet and the youth exchanging hearts is expressed in highly intimate language: The poet assures the youth that he will keep the youth's heart "As tender nurse her babe from faring ill." Such language assumes an exchange of affection, but it also reveals the problem of an older lover trying to dismiss the age difference between himself and his much younger lover. By the sonnet's end, the poet appears overly possessive of the youth: "Presume not on thy heart when mine is slain; / Thou gav'st me thine not to give back again."

- **expiate**   bring to a close.
- **chary**   carefully.

SONNET 23

Most of Sonnet 23 compares the poet's role as a lover to an actor's timidity onstage. The image of the poor theatrical player nervously missing his lines is the first indication that the poet doubts whether his love for the young man is requited.

The first two lines of the sonnet, "As an unperfect actor on the stage,/ Who with his fear is put besides his part," are linked with the first two lines of the second quatrain, "So I, for fear of trust, forget to say/ The perfect ceremony of love's rite." The line "More than that tongue that more hath more expressed" hints at the debased language of a rival poet—like the rival in Sonnet 21. The parallel to this rival poet's abundant language is the poet's excessive love, a passion that, without a doubt, ties his tongue, destroys his confidence, and humbles him.

• **presagers**   indicators.

SONNET 24

When the poet writes in Sonnet 24 of finding "where your true image pictured lies," he focuses on a meaning of "true" in the sense of genuine as opposed to counterfeit. The young man's beauty is often cast as a shape or appearance. Paintings, pictures, visual images, forms, shadows, reflected shapes, and perspective—all of these allude to the impression that the youth's true image is, in fact, a mirage.

Note that the poet's elaborately stylized writing in this sonnet—the first eight lines are an extended metaphor of the poet as a painting onto which the youth's image is painted—is the very kind of writing the poet criticizes elsewhere. But the poet is defining what he sees as he discovers its power over him, almost as if love itself is the creation of a need in oneself where none previously existed.

The poet's gazing at the youth in adoration impresses the image so indelibly upon his heart that the result becomes a private fantasy, totally self-induced, which allows the poet to possess the youth's beauty. In effect, their two personalities are combined. By praising the youth, the poet flatters himself as well. However, the concluding couplet raises doubts once again as to how authentic the poet's depictions of the young man are, and also of how important the young man's physical appearance is as a reflection of his inner feelings and personality. "Yet eyes this cunning want to grace their art" means "But because my eyes see so much beauty in the young man, I want to show his physical appearance most beautifully;" and "They draw but what they see, know not the heart" exposes the limits of the poet's truly getting to know the young man in any way other than through physical attraction. Ultimately, the poet's sonnets are limited in how much of the young man they can portray. The youth is presented as only a surface reality, with no depth of character.

- **stelled**   portrayed.
- **glazed**   paned.

SONNET 25

In Sonnet 25, which has as its theme mortality versus immortality, the poet contrasts himself with those "who are in favor with their stars," implying that, though he is not numbered among those famous, fortunate people, their fame will not last, while his love will. Therefore, he is happy in his love.

Most important, the poet is comforted in the knowledge that his love for the young man grants him permanence: "Then happy I, that love and am beloved / Where I may not remove nor be removed." Requited love between him and the youth replaces his need for fame.

- **rased**   erased.

SONNET 26

Sonnet 26 prepares for the young man's absence from the poet, although the reason for this separation is not clear. The sonnet's first two lines, "Lord of my love, to whom in vassalage / Thy merit hath my duty strongly knit," show the poet's submission to his love, using imagery associated with loyalty and duty to a king. He refers to the sonnet, which represents his duty to the youth who is his king, as "this written ambassage."

In lines 5 through 12, the poet again questions the worth of his poetry, fearful that what he writes about the young man will not be well received. But now he is more worried that the youth himself will reject his poetic advances, whereas before he had consoled himself about his poetic obscurity by recalling the youth's love.

Ironically, the poet's greatest fear, that the youth will reject him, appears to be true, for in the concluding couplet, he concedes that a rift now divides them, and he dares not show his head until the rift is repaired. What is not apparent is what caused this separation. Line 12—"To show me worthy of thy sweet respect"— hints that either the youth has rejected the poet's verses and thus the poet also, or else the poet has removed himself from the relationship until he can rejuvenate his verses to better please the youth. However, the next sonnet sequence (Sonnets 27–32) makes painfully obvious the poet's having left the youth, not the youth's purposefully distancing himself from the poet.

- **vassalage**   servitude.

- **ambassage**   message.

- **aspect**   astrological term for influence.

- **prove**   test.

SONNET 27

The poet describes himself as being "weary with toil" and trying to sleep. The somber mood announces a new phase in the relationship. In the first four lines, the poet likens his state of mind to traveling afar. Restlessly, he cannot sleep because his mind is filled with thoughts of the youth: "Lo, thus, by day my limbs, by night my mind, / For thee and for myself no quiet find."

With Sonnet 27, the poet seems to regard the youth's affection less securely. Their absence from each other signals a coolness in the relationship. The physical distance, however, does not dull the youth's alluring beauty; the poet imagines the young man as a blinding, brilliant jewel. In line 10, the poet's seeing the youth's "shadow" makes their relationship seem more tenuous, for "shadow" in this context represents the youth's image, which no longer has substance.

SONNET 28

Images of absence, continued from the previous sonnet, show the poet at the point of emotional exhaustion and frustration due to his sleepless nights spent thinking about the young man. However, even though faced with the young man's disinterest, the poet still refuses to break away from the youth. He even continues to praise the youth, telling day and night how fortunate they are to be graced by the youth's presence. The poet's continued devotion to the young man is not so startling as it might first appear: Writing sonnets of absolute devotion in Elizabethan times was a duty to the source of the poet's inspiration. Sonnet 28, therefore, offers the poet's verse as a duty-offering, a supreme expression of selfless love for an undeserving friend. The opposition between day and night dominates the sonnet. For the poet, neither time alleviates his suffering: "And each, though enemies to either's reign, / Do in consent shake hands to torture me" with hard work and no sleep. Trying to please the oppressive day and night, the poet tells day that the youth shines brightly even when the sun is hidden; to night, the poet compares the youth to the brightest stars, except that the youth shines even when the stars do not. However, day and night still torment the poet and make "grief's strength seem stronger." The poet sinks even further into despair.

- **swart-complexioned**   dark-complected; swarthy.
- **twire**   peek.
- **gild'st the even**   make the evening bright.

SONNET 29

Resenting his bad luck, the poet envies the successful art of others and rattles off an impressive catalogue of the ills and misfortunes of his life. His depression is derived from his being separated from the young man, even more so because he envisions the youth in the company of others while the poet is "all alone."

Stylistically, Sonnet 29 is typically Shakespearean in its form. The first eight lines, which begin with "When," establish a conditional argument and show the poet's frustration with his craft. The last six lines, expectedly beginning in line 9 with "Yet"—similar to other sonnets' "But"—and resolving the conditional argument, present a splendid image of a morning lark that "sings hymns at heaven's gate." This image epitomizes the poet's delightful memory of his friendship with the youth and compensates for the misfortunes he has lamented.

The uses of "state" unify the sonnet's three different sections: the first eight lines, lines 9 through 12, and the concluding couplet, lines 13 and 14. Additionally, the different meanings of state—as a mood and as a lot in life—contrast the poet's sense of a failed and defeated life to his exhilaration in recalling his friendship with the youth. One state, as represented in lines 2 and 14, is his state of life; the other, in line 10, is his state of mind. Ultimately, although the poet plaintively wails his "outcast state" in line 2, by the end of the sonnet he has completely reversed himself: ". . . I scorn to change my state with kings." Memories of the young man rejuvenate his spirits.

- **bootless** useless.
- **haply** perhaps.

SONNET 30

The poet repeats Sonnet 29's theme, that memories of the youth are priceless compensations—not only for many disappointments and unrealized hopes but for the loss of earlier friends: "But if the while I think on thee, dear friend, / All losses are restored and sorrows end." Stylistically, Sonnet 30 identically mirrors the preceding sonnet's poetic form.

This sonnet is one of the most exquisitely crafted in the entire sequence dealing with the poet's depression over the youth's separation (Sonnets 26–32). It includes an extraordinary complexity of sound patterns, including the effective use of alliteration—repetitive consonant sounds in a series of words—for example, both the "s" and "t" sounds in "sessions of sweet silent thought."

But alliteration is only one method poets use to enhance the melody of their work. Rhyme, of course, is another device for doing this. A third is assonance—similar vowel sounds in accented syllables—for example, the short "e" sound in the phrases "When sessions" and "remembrance". In this case, the short "e" sound helps unify the sonnet, for the assonant sound both begins—"When"—and concludes—"end"—the sonnet.

Contributing to the distinctive rhythm of Sonnet 30's lines is the variation of accents in the normally iambic pentameter lines.

For example, line 7 has no obvious alternation of short and long syllables. Equal stress is placed on "weep afresh love's long," with only slightly less stress on "since," which follows this phrase. Likewise, in line 6, "friends hid" and "death's dateless night" are equally stressed. This sonnet typifies why the Shakespeare of the sonnets is held to be without rival in achieving rhythm, melody, and sound within the limited sonnet structure.

SONNET 31

Sonnet 31 expands upon the sentiment conveyed in the preceding sonnet's concluding couplet, "But if the while I think on thee, dear friend, / All losses are restored and sorrows end." In the present sonnet, the young man is a microcosm representing all the poet's past lovers and friends; however, the poet's separation from the youth also represents the loss of companionship with these now-dead lovers and friends. Ironically, the young man, whom the poet earlier admonished to bear children to stave off death and mortality, now himself becomes an image of death: "Thou art the grave where buried love doth live."

The sonnet demonstrates that the poet is really writing to himself rather than to the young man. His physical separation from the youth prompts him to remember lost loves and then link them to his current relationship with the youth. The poet rejoices that his dead friends are metaphysically implanted in the youth's bosom, but lost friends and lovers—not the young man—are the main subjects of the sonnet.

SONNET 32

Sonnet 32 concludes the sonnet sequence on the poet's depression over his absence from the youth. Again the poet questions the worth of his poems, but this time his insecurity has to do with their style and not with the intensity of their subject matter, which is his love for the youth: "Reserve them for my love, not for their rhyme." The thoughts of his friends' and lovers' deaths in the previous sonnet make the poet reflect on his own mortality. Envisioning what the young man will say about the sonnets years hence, the poet expects the surviving youth to read them and deem them old-fashioned, so he asks that the youth read them for the love the poet had for him rather than for their style. There is a charming modesty to the poet's self-effacing attitude, but his tone is depressed and resentful of his unhappiness.

• **bett'ring**   improvement as time passes.

SONNET 33

Sonnet 33 begins a new phase in the poet and youth's estrangement from each other. (The breach well may be caused by the youth's seduction of the poet's mistress, which the poet addresses in later sonnets.) In any case, faith between the two men is broken during the poet's absence.

Shifts in the poet's attitudes toward the youth and about his own involvement in the relationship are evident in the sonnet. Whereas in Sonnet 25 the poet boasts that his faith is permanent, here he reverses himself. References to "basest clouds," "ugly rack," "stealing," "disgrace," and "stain" indicate that the friend has committed a serious moral offense. Whereas in earlier sonnets the poet worried that his verse was not good enough to convey his intense love for the young man, now he worries about whether the young man is as good as his verse conveyed. Metaphorically, the young man is like the sun, which "with golden face" warms and brightens the earth. However, the sun allows "the basest clouds" to block its rays, and the young man permits loyalties to other people to interfere with his relationship with the poet. The poet accepts that the friend has betrayed him—"But, out alack, he was but one hour mine"—but he also realizes that the burden of blame must be his own for having assumed that outward beauty corresponds to inner virtue. This last realization, that outward beauty does *not* correspond to inner virtue, is expressed in the sonnet's last line: "Suns of the world may stain when heaven's sun staineth." In other words, "Suns of the world may stain"—perhaps a pun on "sons" or humankind—represents the young man's moral transgression although his external, physical appearance remains unchanged. Nevertheless, the poet's love for the young man remains unchanged.

- **alchemy** to turn something into gold.
- **anon** soon.
- **rack** a mass of streaming clouds.

SONNET 34

The poet speaks of a quite different feeling than he did in Sonnet 33. He is puzzled and painfully disappointed by the youth, whose callousness dashes any hope of his enjoying a dependable friendship. The opening complaint, again based on the metaphor of the young man as the sun, shows how much the poet's perceptions have changed. He has been wounded by the youth, and apologies notwithstanding, the scar remains: "For no man well of such a salve can speak / That heals the wound, and cures not the disgrace."

The poet might lament the inner hurt that he feels because of the youth's actions, but the sonnet ends with him unable to remain angry. Just as in Sonnet 33's line 13, "Yet him for this my love no whit disdaineth," the poet remains steadfast in his devotion to the youth. Although disgraced because of the youth's actions, the poet in the concluding couplet forgives his friend: "Ah, but those tears are pearl which thy love sheeds, / And they are rich and ransom all ill deeds." The young man apparently cries because of his offense against the poet and effectively manipulates the poet's sentiments so that the poet forgives him for jeopardizing their relationship.

- **physic** remedy.
- **sheeds** sheds.

SONNET 35

Whereas in Sonnet 33 the poet is an onlooker, in the previous sonnet and here in Sonnet 35, the poet recognizes his own contribution to the youth's wrongdoing in the excuses that he has made for the youth over time. Sonnet 35 begins with parallel objects that, although beautiful, contain some sort of imperfection: "Roses have thorns, and silver fountains mud." Likewise, clouds, which are a recurring image in the sonnets concerning moral transgressions, darken both night and day, additional favorite images used by the poet. The poet therefore absolves the young man and defends the youth's betrayal.

What is most striking in Sonnet 35 is not that the poet forgives the youth but that the poet actually blames *himself* for the youth's betrayal more than he does the young man. That he finds himself guilty is emphasized by the legal terminology incorporated in the sonnet: "Thy adverse party is thy advocate—/ And 'gainst myself a lawful plea commence." The poet admits that he made too much out of the youth's absence from him; he now knows that he overreacted, in part because "Such civil war is in my love and hate." However, if the poet thinks that he can rid himself of this "civil war" simply by acknowledging its existence, the remaining sonnets prove him wrong.

SONNET 36

Obstacles to the friendship between the poet and the young man remain, but the poet is no longer wholly duped by his young friend. However, he still maintains that their love for one another is as strong as ever: "Let me confess that we two must be twain / Although our undivided loves are one." What is more clear than ever, though, is that the poet is wrong.

The poet's indifference to the youth's continued misbehavior—"those blots"—turns to open scorn, not of the youth, but rather of having to remain publicly separated from him. The necessity of a separation—"separable spite"—is a decision born of hard-won wisdom. Public shame makes the poet desire to bear his suffering alone, publicly refraining from acknowledging the young man—"I may not evermore acknowledge thee, / . . . / Nor thou with public kindness honor me." What is painfully apparent is that the poet has been publicly ridiculed and that the young man deceitfully continues to court favor from others. At this point in the sonnets, the relationship between the two men seems one-sided and incredibly unfair.

• **twain**   two separate beings.

SONNET 37

Sonnet 37, which echoes Sonnet 36, conveys the emotions of a doting parent and discontinues the confessional mode of the previous sonnets. "As a decrepit father takes delight / To see his active child do deeds of youth," the poet takes comfort in the youth's superlative qualities, and wishes "what is best," for the youth. If the youth then has the best, the poet will be ten times happier. Separated from the young man, the poet now is content merely to hear other people's favorable opinions of the youth: "So I, made lame by Fortune's dearest spite, / Take all my comfort of thy worth and truth." Sadly, the poet seems to be living *through* the young man rather than *for* himself.

SONNET 38

Like the previous sonnet, Sonnet 38 contrasts the selfishly lascivious youth and the adoring, idealistic poet. The poet appears pitifully unable to contemplate his life without the youth, who remains physically distanced from the poet. The poet's emotional reliance on the young man dominates the sonnet. For example, the youth provides the inspiration for the poet's verse: "How can my Muse want subject to invent / While thou dost breathe." The youth is even hailed as the "tenth Muse," generating ten times the inspiration of the other nine. Ironically, the poet demeans the worth of his own verse not only by acknowledging his complete reliance on the young man but by admitting that any poet could write exceptional poetry were the young man the poem's subject matter.

The poet basks in his good fortune, but he is not optimistic about the success of his verse: "If my slight Muse do please these curious days, / The pain be mine, but thine shall be the praise." He continues to bear all of the responsibility for the relationship's success or failure, but he seems to be so wholly submerged in his affections for the young man that he risks losing sympathy for his plight.

SONNET 39

Sonnet 39 constructs an ingenious variation on the theme of absence. Ironically, separation is inspirational: "That by this separation

I may give / That due to thee which thou deserv'st alone." Also, as the youth is the "better part" of the poet, the two remain united through the poet's imagination, though they are physically separated. Through a series of rhetorical questions, the poet explores the paradox of his being simultaneously two beings. There can be no satisfactory conclusion as separate lives make separate identities, not one. Either the poet loves himself and betrays the youth, or the poet loves the youth and betrays himself.

SONNET 40

Sonnet 40 begins a three-sonnet sequence in which the poet shares his possessions and his mistress with the youth, although it is not until Sonnet 41 that he directly mentions their liaison.

The use of the word "love" may be confusing to readers, for "love" in this sonnet means at least three different things. Two of these meanings are addressed in the first line, "Take all my loves, my love, yea, take them all." Here, "my loves" refers to the poet's possessions, both physical—the sonnets themselves—and emotional. Following this, the phrase "my love," set off by commas, refers to the young man himself, whom the poet is addressing. Although the allusion to the youth's now possessing the poet's mistress is slight in this sonnet, line 6—"I cannot blame thee for my love thou usest"—contains the strongest hint of this new relationship: The young man "usest" the poet's mistress—"my love."

In an almost pathetically timid voice, the poet wavers between anger at and forgiveness of the young man. Line 7 begins, "But yet be blamed," and we expect the poet to rant in extreme hostility at the youth, but this mood then shifts to the forgiveness contained in lines 9 and 10: "I do forgive thy robb'ry, gentle thief, / Although thou steal thee all my poverty." In lines 11 and 12, the mood shifts again, but now the poet waxes philosophically about the contrasts between love and hate: ". . . it is a greater grief / To bear love's wrong than hate's known injury." And finally, even while angry over the affair, the poet forgives the youth's lecherous nature: "Lascivious grace, in whom all ill well shows, / Kill me with spites; yet we must not be foes."

SONNET 41

In order to forgive the youth for his actions, the poet places himself in both the youth's position and that of the mistress. In the sonnet's first four lines, the poet mildly accuses the young man of committing small sins, but he then goes on to accept the youth's actions given his age and beauty. The youth's behavior, so the poet seems to say, is natural and expected. However, what is even more expected is that others attempt to gain the young man's affections: "Beauteous thou art, therefore to be assailed." This reasoning prompts the poet to blame those who tempt the youth rather than the youth himself.

Forgiveness of the young man is mixed with reprimand, for he breaks "a twofold truth"—the poet and the mistress' affair—when he begins loving the woman. Although the poet admonishes the youth, his tone is reserved, in part because he suggests that the youth and the youth's beauty are two separate things: "And chide thy beauty and thy straying youth, / Who lead thee in their riot even there / Where thou art forced to break a twofold truth." The young man is not at fault for coming between the poet and the mistress; rather, his beauty and youth "forced" him to act as he did.

SONNET 42

Only in this last sonnet concerning the youth and the poet's mistress does the poet make fully apparent the main reason for his being so upset: "That she hath thee is of my wailing chief, / A loss in love that touches me more nearly." The poet is grieved by his mistress' infidelity, but he laments even more the fact that she has what he so ravenously craves: the physical and emotional attentions of the young man.

Reconciling himself to his mistress' behavior requires all the poet's powers of expression and self-deception. He makes the torturous argument that since he and the youth share personalities, they must share the same woman: "But here's the joy: my friend and I are one; / Sweet flattery! then she loves but me alone." Likewise, because the poet loves the woman, and because the woman is having an affair with the young man, then the rational conclusion—according to the poet—is that the poet and the youth are that much closer in *their* relationship.

SONNET 43

The next sonnet series on absence begins here with Sonnet 43 and continues through Sonnet 58. Throughout this new sequence, different meanings of the same words are developed in versatile constructions and juxtapositions. Note the curious double use of "shadow" and "form" in "Then thou, whose shadow shadows doth make bright, / How would thy shadow's form form happy show . . ." Three rhyme links to Sonnet 44 —"so"/ "slow," "stay"/"stay," and "thee"/"thee"—reveal a closely unified theme. Also, "darkly bright . . . bright in dark" in Sonnet 43 is echoed in "bright," "light," "night," "sightless," "nights," and "night's bright" in the other sonnets. In Sonnet 43, the poet surmises that his only consolation in being separated from the youth is at night, when he can dream of the youth's beauty. Images of reversal are prevalent, and all of them address how the young man affects the poet. For example, the poet says that at night he is content because he best sees the youth in his dreams: The youth—a "shade"—casts off light that illuminates his beauty. But during the day, the poet grieves, for then the youth's absence is most acute. These paradoxical situations between day and night and between the youth's presence and absence are most fully described in the sonnet's concluding couplet: "All days are nights to see till I see thee, / And nights bright days when dreams do show thee me." The poet's world is upside down.

SONNET 44

Sonnet 44 and the following one form a continuous theme involving the four basic elements of matter according to Elizabethan science: earth, water, air, and fire. Sonnet 44 deals with earth and water, and Sonnet 45 with air and fire.

In Sonnet 44, the poet laments his physical distance from the young man. He argues that if his body were made of only thoughts, then all he would have to do is think about the youth and they would be together. However, although the poet's mind is free to travel, he fails to come to grips with any tangible reality in the youth.

SONNET 45

This sonnet continues and completes the idea of Sonnet 44, but here air and fire—symbolizing the poet's thoughts and desires, respectively—are linked to the youth because the poet continuously thinks about and desires the young man. Figuratively, the sonnet implies not so much direct communication as the telepathic exchange of emotions. Alone, the poet "sinks down to death, oppressed with melancholy," and does not recover until the youth sends his well-wishes and love back to him. However, the poet's melancholic emotions are cyclical, for as soon as the young man sends back these greetings, the poet begins to think about and to desire the youth, and shortly he feels alone again.

SONNET 46

The poet alludes to contradictions within himself when he considers his longing for the sight of the youth's good looks and his need to love and be loved by the youth himself. Sonnet 46 thus deals with the theme of conflict between the poet's eyes and heart: "Mine eye and heart are at a mortal war / How to divide the conquest of thy sight." He says that his heart wants the youth to itself, and the eye would bar the heart from the youth as well. Legal terminology used in the sonnet reflects contemporary life in the impaneling of an impartial jury to decide the matter. A verdict is reached when the poet awards the youth's outward appearance to the eye and his inner love to the heart.

• **moity** share.

SONNET 47

In Sonnet 46, conflict between the eyes and heart is the theme. In Sonnet 47, these organs complement one another. The sonnet, rather uninspired compared to many of Shakespeare's sonnets, contrasts the actual and imaginary youth: "So, either by thy picture or my love, / Thyself away are present still with me." When the poet grows melancholy for the young man, he simply looks at the youth's image, and his love for his friend is rejuvenated.

SONNET 48

The youth keeps the poet on edge, and once again we see the poet's bondage to the relationship. The poet develops a metaphorical contrast between being robbed of physical possessions and losing emotional ties to the young man. This loss that he so fears is already in the making, and only *he* seems unable to recognize the youth's growing rejection of him. "Thee have I not locked up in any chest," he says to the youth, but then he mitigates this thought by continuing, "Save where thou art not, though I feel thou art, / Within the gentle closure of my breast . . ." The self-contradiction lies in the poet's acknowledging the youth's emotional distance from him but then refusing to believe this truth.

Of greatest concern to the poet is the youth's inability to protect himself from scurrilous suitors. Even the poet's mistress comes under fire: As the object of her affection, the youth is "the prey of every vulgar thief." This reference to thievery unites the sonnet, for in line 4 the poet speaks of "hands of falsehood," and the concluding couplet more directly addresses the poet's greatest fear: "And even thence thou wilt be stol'n, I fear, / For truth proves thievish for a prize so dear." Ironically, here the poet seems most worried that his complete acceptance of the fact that the youth is spurning him will be the greatest—and most fearful—"truth" of all.

SONNET 49

All pride is missing in this sonnet, whose first four lines continue the poet's fear of the "truth" evoked in the preceding sonnet. Moreover, the poet is prepared to place blame on himself for the youth's no longer loving him: "And this my hand against myself uprear . . ." In this carefully structured poem, there is no mistaking the poet's humility and sadness, indicated especially in the repeated phrase "Against that time" at the beginning of each quatrain. The first two instances of this phrase describe the youth's future desertion; the third defends it. Writing of the young man, the poet accepts the inevitable time "when thou shalt strangely pass"; he shall scarcely blame the youth for leaving "poor me."

SONNET 50

Nothing suggests where the poet is journeying in this and the following sonnets. All that is known is that the poet is on an unnamed journey away from the young man. The poet's allusion to solitude has no definite time frame, and the journey may be brief. However, the youth is the standard against whom the poet measures everything, so it is not surprising when the poet says, "Thus far the miles are measured from thy friend."

The poet draws an analogy between himself and the beast on which he rides: "The beast that bears me, tired with my woe, / Plods dully on, to bear that weight in me," as though the non-physical weight of the poet's sadness factors into the burden that the beast must carry. Similarly, the groan that the animal makes prompts the poet to recall his own sad state in traveling farther away from the youth: "For that same groan doth put this in my mind: / My grief lies onward and my joy behind." Here, "onward" means physically forward, but it also means into the future. Because this future doesn't involve the young man, the poet is grieved. Likewise, "behind" means from where the poet physically has traveled, but it also means the past, which was joyful because the poet had the affections of the youth.

SONNET 51

The companion to the previous sonnet, Sonnet 51 further expands on the theme of traveling. Many of the details in Sonnet 50 appear here, including the "slow offence / Of my dull bearer," which mirrors "The beast . . . / Plods dully on," and the relative weight of different emotions: the heavy weight of sadness in the previous sonnet compared to the light, effervescent weight of desire in Sonnet 51.

Sonnet 51 mixes the present with the future—what the poet termed "onward" in the last line of the previous sonnet. The first four lines occur in the present, but line 4's "Till I return" prompts the poet to think about the future. However, unlike the grievous future in Sonnet 50, this future is joyful, for the poet believes that his thoughts of love for the young man will accelerate his return: "Then can no horse with my desire keep pace." Note that this

48

desire is characterized as "fiery," which recalls Sonnet 45, in which the poet imagined desire as a "purging fire."

SONNET 52

The poet grows more accepting of his separation from the young man, whom he likens to "up-lockèd treasure." This image of the youth as a treasure unites the sonnet: In line 9, the poet writes, "So is the time that keeps you as my chest," "chest" clearly referring to the locked treasure that is the youth. Also, the terms "imprisoned" in line 12 and "up-lockèd" are similarly linked.

Finally realizing that separation from the young man has its advantages, the poet deems it a blessing in disguise that he and the youth meet infrequently—encounters that he characterizes as "feasts so solemn and so rare." The fewer meetings between the two, the more special and intensely emotional are those rendezvous.

- **carcanet** jewelled collar.

SONNET 53

A more relaxed poet appears to have forgotten his previous doubts about his relationship with the young man, who is still attractive but whose true self is elusive. Ironically, the poet's lavish and ornate eulogy of the youth—for example, when he compares him to Adonis, a legendary classical beauty—is exactly the kind of affected, stilted, and insincere-sounding poetry which the poet earlier criticized his rivals for indulging in.

The extravagance of the poet's figures of speech hints at an illusory creature, subtle and complex, perhaps beyond the poet's powers to describe. Images of shadows, shades, and painting run throughout the sonnet, and the poet's language employs ambiguous terms—for example, "shadow" may mean silhouette, picture, reflection, symbol, or ghost. Other abstract terms are "substance," "tires," and "blessed shape." Such language indicates the indefinable, cryptic nature of the youth.

- **foison** abundant harvest.
- **tires** attire.

SONNET 54

The rose image in this sonnet symbolizes immortal truth and devotion, two virtues that the poet associates with the young man. Likening himself to a distiller, the poet, who argues that his verse distills the youth's beauty, or "truth," sees poetry as a procreative activity: Poetry alone creates an imperishable image of the youth.

Stylistically, the sonnet's form follows the now-familiar model of most of the sonnets, with lines 1 through 8 establishing an argument or situation, and lines 9 through 12, beginning with "But," contrasting that original argument or situation. The first four lines describe how a rose is outwardly beautiful, but its beauty extends to the "sweet odor which doth in it live." Likewise, lines 5 through 8 describe canker blooms as also being externally beautiful. The dissimilarity between these two flowers, however, is evident in lines 9 through 12, in which the poet notes that canker blooms contain no inner beauty. Unlike roses, which "Of their sweet deaths are sweetest odors made," canker blooms leave no such lasting impression when they die: "They live unwooed and unrespected fade, / Die to themselves."

The concluding couplet makes clear the poet's purpose for this extended botany lesson. The young man is like the rose, outwardly beautiful and inwardly sweet-smelling, two qualities that the poet characterizes as the youth's "truth"; the poet's sonnets are similar to the perfume made from dead roses, for after the youth's beauty fades, the poet's verse "distills"—immortalizes—that former beauty for others to enjoy.

- **canker blooms**   dog-roses.
- **vade**   depart.

SONNET 55

Sonnet 55, one of Shakespeare's most famous verses, asserts the immortality of the poet's sonnets to withstand the forces of decay over time. The sonnet continues this theme from the previous sonnet, in which the poet likened himself to a distiller of truth.

Although the poet's previous pride in writing verse is missing in this sonnet, he still manages to demonstrate a superbly confident spirit: "Not marble, nor the gilded monuments / Of princes, shall outlive this powerful rime." He clearly abandons, at least for the time being, his earlier depressing opinion of his verse as "barren rime," for next he contrasts his verses' immortality to "unswept stone, besmeared with sluttish time," meaning that the young man will be remembered longer because of the poet's having written about him than if descriptions of his beauty had been chiseled in stone.

The next four lines address the same theme of immortality, but now the poet boasts that not only natural forces but human wars and battles cannot blot out his sonnets, which are a "living record" of the youth. Monuments and statues may be desecrated during war, but not so these rhymes.

In the first seventeen sonnets, the poet worried about death's effect on the youth's beauty and questioned the nature of his sonnets' reputation after both he and the young man died. Now, however, in lines 9 through 12, he boldly asserts that death is impotent in the face of his sonnets' immortality: To the youth he says, "Gainst death and all-oblivious enmity / Shall you pace forth." In fact, he asserts that the young man's name will be remembered until the last survivor on earth perishes: ". . . your praise shall still find room / Even in the eyes of all posterity / That wear this world out to the ending doom." Only then, when no one remains alive, will the youth's beauty fade—but through no fault of the youth or the poet.

This notion of "the ending doom" is the main point in the concluding couplet. The syntax of line 13—"So, till the judgment that yourself arise"—is confusing; restated, the line says, "Until the Judgment Day when you arise." The poet assures the youth that his beauty will remain immortal as long as one single person still lives to read these sonnets, which themselves will be immortal.

- **sluttish** untidy.
- **broils** battles.

SONNET 56

Much like in Sonnet 52, the poet accepts that separation can be advantageous in making their love that much sweeter when the youth and the poet resume their relationship. The poet asks the abstract love to be renewed so that he can be reunited with the youth. He begs, "Sweet love, renew thy force," and likens this "sad interim" to an ocean that separates two shores, whereon two lovers stand, hoping to catch a glimpse of each other and increase their love. Or else, the poet says, consider this "dulness" a winter, which implies the coming of summer and makes that coming all the more wished for. The sonnet has a sad, wistful tone as the poet seeks a way to rekindle the love that bound their relationship.

• **contracted new**   newly betrothed.

SONNET 57

In Sonnet 57, the poet argues that he is not so much the young man's friend as he is his slave. As a slave, he waits on the youth's pleasure: "But, like a sad slave, stay and think of nought / Save where you are how happy you make those." Annoyed and sad underneath his dignified and polite phrasing, the poet seems to be losing the ability to think and judge critically: "So true a fool is love that in your will, / Though you do anything, he thinks no ill." Ironically, these last two lines read more true if we substitute the poet for the word "love" and its pronoun "he": "So true a fool am I in your will, / Though you do anything, I think no ill." Following so closely after the soaring verse of Sonnet 55, the poet's quick descent into self-pity makes his situation even more pathetic.

SONNET 58

As in so many other sonnets, the poet's annoyance with the young man is expressed ambiguously. We hardly notice that he rebukes the youth in the lines "That god forbid that made me first your slave / I should in thought control your times of pleasure." Surely the suggestion is that the poet will not complain of his neglect: "And patience, tame to sufferance, bide each check / Without

52

accusing you of injury." Nor does he expect an accounting of the youth's time. Still, an injury is implied: "I am to wait, though waiting so be hell, / Not blame your pleasure, be it ill or well." Moreover, "self-doing crime" implies that the youth hurts not only the poet but himself as well. If nothing else, however, the poet's dignity is slighted.

SONNET 59

Sonnet 59 dwells on the paradox that what is new is always expressed in terms of what is already known. The elements of any invention or creative composition must be common knowledge, or old news. The phrase "laboring for invention" indicates not only the poet's determination to create something entirely new in his verse but also his frustration in trying to do so.

Once again questioning the worth of his sonnets, the poet longs for the chance to read verse written about beauty such as the young man's "Even of five hundred courses of the sun." He wants to judge his sonnets against those of antiquity—"the old world"—to determine if he is simply rehashing what has already been written about beauty. But even more than this, he wants to confirm that his sonnets are as good, if not better, than other poetry whose subject is beauty. He ends stating that he's certain that previous writers have given high praise to lesser subjects than the beautiful youth.

SONNET 60

Sonnet 60 is acknowledged as one of Shakespeare's greatest because it deals with the universal concerns of time and its passing. In the sonnet, time is symbolized by concrete images. For example, the opening two lines present a simile in which time is represented by "waves" and "minutes": "Like as the waves make towards the pebbled shore, / So do our minutes hasten to their end"; here, death is "the pebbled shore"—another concrete image.

In the second quatrain, the poet laments time's unfairness. A child—"Nativity"—is born and, over time, matures to adulthood, and yet the adult now dreads the maturation process as he grows increasingly older and thus reaches the point of death, or the end of time. Time, which gives life, now takes it away: "And Time that gave doth now his gift confound."

The antithesis in lines 9 through 12 is between the aging poet and the youth's good looks. The poet warns, "Time doth transfix the flourish set on youth / And delves the parallels in beauty's brow." In other words, the young man currently is beautiful, but "parallels"—wrinkles—will eventually appear, as they have on the poet. However much the young man and the poet would like beauty to reside forever on the youth's face, "nothing stands but for his [time's] scythe to mow."

Nonetheless, the poet promises to immortalize the youth's good looks before time's wrinkles appear on his face: "And yet to times in hope my verse shall stand, / Praising thy worth, despite his cruel hand." Unlike the poet's promise in Sonnet 19, this assurance does not include giving the young man eternal beauty. Even more, the "scythe" in line 12 recalls Sonnet 12's concluding couplet: "And nothing 'gainst Time's scythe can make defense / Save breed, to brave him when he takes thee hence." Clearly the poet is no longer concerned that the young man have a child to ensure the immortality of his beauty. Now, the poet's own sonnets are the only security the youth needs to gain eternal worth.

SONNET 61

The youth continues to present a variety of phantom images to the poet. Trying to settle on one authentic image, the poet cannot sleep because of the emotional turmoil caused by his obsession with the youth. Shapes and visions of the youth are the disembodied "shadows like to thee"—shadows that frustrate the poet and prevent him from concluding anything about the youth. This theme recalls earlier sonnets in which the poet battled sleep and wakefulness.

The poet seems more than a little paranoid that the youth will think ill of him. In the second quatrain, he originally asks if the youth purposefully sends his "spirit" to upset the poet, "To find out shames and idle hours in me." However, the next four lines make clear that the cause of the poet's misery is his own affection for the youth and not the youth's for him: "O no, thy love, though much, is not so great; / It is my love that keeps mine eye awake." Fearful that his intense love may embarrass or shame the object of his affection, the poet attempts to regulate his own emotions—for the youth's sake, not for his own: "Mine own true love that doth my rest defeat / To play the watchman ever for thy sake." The poet is left with watching the youth from afar, wanting to hoard the young man's attention but unable to do so. The phrase "with others all too near" demonstrates that the poet is not at all pleased that the young man is receiving the affections of other suitors, affections the poet feels are his—and only his—to give.

SONNET 62

The poet thinks of himself as a young man and condemns his own narcissistic vanity. Unfortunately, although he can intellectualize narcissism as an unworthy attribute, nonetheless "It is so grounded inward in my heart."

This youthful image of himself is abruptly shattered in lines 9 through 12, beginning with the typical "But," when the poet looks at himself in a mirror and sees his true self, "Beated and chopped with tanned antiquity." Swinging between this antithesis of youth and old age, the poet's narcissistic self-love makes him guilty of his young friend's vice: "Tis thee, myself, that for myself I praise, / Painting my age with beauty of thy days." While he condemns vanity in the youth, he admires it in himself. The phrase "for myself" means that he has assumed the youth's identity, and the problem of the youth's identity remains one of vanity. As is evident in later sonnets, the poet is preoccupied with the idea of personal identity.

SONNET 63

References to the young man's future are signs of the poet's fear that love cannot defend against time. The youth could die— "When hours have drained his blood"—and so could his beauty— "And all those beauties whereof now he's king / Are vanishing, or vanished out of sight"—but when the youth is as aged as the poet, the youth's former good looks will be preserved in the poet's verse. "Confounding age's cruel knife," which recalls Sonnet 60's "And Time that gave doth now his gift confound," is no match against the poet's sonnets, "these black lines" in which the young man will forever live "still green."

SONNET 64

In Sonnet 64, the poet is portrayed as a historian, philosopher, and antiquarian who dreams of time's relentless destruction of ancient glories. Monuments that reflect the noblest ideas of humankind—castles, churches, and cities—will one day be "confounded to decay."

Sonnet 64 is remarkably similar to Sonnet 60, yet each sonnet concludes in a very different tone. Many of the same images are found in both sonnets: the ocean's tireless pounding of the shore; the give-and-take battle between water and the land; and the use of the word "confound" to characterize time's ceaseless progress. However, whereas Sonnet 60's concluding couplet evokes feelings of high-spirited joy and confidence, Sonnet 64 ends in despair: The poet is now certain that death will "take my love away," but he no longer seems satisfied that his verse will ensure the youth's immortality. The sonnet's last two lines convey a grievous, depressing tone: "This thought is as a death, which cannot choose / But weep to have that which it fears to lose." The poet finally acknowledges the youth's—and his own—mortality.

SONNET 65

Continuing many of the images from Sonnet 64, the poet concludes that nothing withstands time's ravages. The hardest metals and stones, the vast earth and sea—all submit to time "Since brass, nor stone, nor earth, nor boundless sea, / But sad mortality o'ersways their power." "O fearful meditation!" he cries, where can the young man hide that time won't wreak on him the same "siege of batt'ring days"?

In contrast to the previous sonnet, the poet once again is reassured that his sonnets will provide the youth immortality—his verse is the only thing that can withstand time's decay. Returning to the power of poetry to bestow eternal life, the poet asserts "That in black ink my love may still shine bright." He believes that his love verse can preserve the youth's beauty. Ironically, this back-and-forth thinking mirrors the movement of the waves to the shore—an image the poet uses in many of the time-themed sonnets in this sequence.

For example, in Sonnet 60, the poet says, "Each changing place with that which goes before, / In sequent toil all forwards do contend"; and in Sonnet 64, he notes, "Increasing store with loss and loss with store." Physically and emotionally separated from the young man, the poet's constantly shifting belief in the worth of his verse parallels his constantly shifting faith in the young man.

SONNET 66

Were it not that dying would take him from his love, the angry speaker of this litany of life's disappointments would die. Everywhere he sees the undeserving win public esteem—"And gilded honor shamefully misplaced"—while the virtuous and needy are neglected, or even worse, disgraced. However, the poet thinks that the youth would suffer by his demise. Therefore, he puts up with life's disappointments and the public criticism of his life and art: "Tired with all these, from these would I be gone, / Save that, to die, I leave my love alone."

SONNET 67

Sonnet 67 continues the thought of the previous sonnet, and develops a new argument in its reflection upon the poet's contemporary age. Although the poet still professes faith in the youth's natural endowments, he is put out of sorts by the public rage for artificial beauty in life and art: "Why should false painting imitate his cheek / And steal dead seeing of his living hue?" What's more, he wonders why the young man would submit himself to such false treatment. The youth is the standard of beauty against which everything else is measured: "Why should poor beauty indirectly seek / Roses of shadow, since his rose is true?" Natural beauty needs no cosmetics, yet the youth subjects himself to impostor artists who alter his appearance by false means.

- **dead seeing** lifeless appearance.
- **bankrout** bankrupt.

SONNET 68

Because the young man epitomizes ancient standards of true beauty, he does not need cosmetics or a wig made from "the golden tresses of the dead." In these sonnets, the poet exhibits a general tendency to censure poetic extravagance and to identify such lavishness with the youth's false friends, as well as with the cosmetic vogue, which the poet castigates as "bastard signs of fair." So the poet invokes the natural beauty—"Without all ornament, itself and true"—of classical times.

Sonnet 68 and the previous sonnet are more concerned with the poet's criticism of his cultural age than criticism of the young man. Perhaps because the poet has been spurned by this cultural age, he retaliates against other artists and poets. Or perhaps because the definition of beauty is changing, the poet fears that the young man will no longer be seen as the standard of beauty; his own sonnets will then be viewed as old, stale, outdated verse. Whatever the reason, the poet strongly condemns this general decline in what is perceived as beautiful. For the poet, the young man remains natural beauty, while the contemporary world is "false Art."

- **bastard signs** cosmetics.
- **fair** beauty.

SONNET 69

Although the youth's enemies praise his appearance, they all but slander him in their private meetings. Contrasting the youth's outward beauty—"Those parts of thee that the world's eye doth view"—to his deeds, the poet, in a rare display of independence, criticizes his young friend. His argument is well-founded: Because the youth associates with these reckless and wasteful men who slander him behind his back, he must assume their vices. Recalling Sonnet 54, in which the poet discusses the beauty and sweet odor of roses, the poet asks the youth why he no longer has the rose's sweet smell. Surprisingly, his own answer is curt and unsympathetic: "But why thy odor matcheth not thy show, / The soil is this, that thou dost common grow." Because the youth associates with disreputable persons, he is becoming disreputable himself, more like a smelly weed than a rose.

SONNET 70

The poet is unable to maintain his disapproval of the young man, but he forgives without forgetting. The youth can blame only himself for the slanderous rumors about him. The poet notes that the slander pays an oblique and unintended tribute to the youth's innocence, charm, and beauty: "For canker vice the sweetest buds doth love, / And thou present'st a pure unstained prime." The youth's real problem, according to the poet, is that his morally ambiguous nature leaves him vulnerable to slander; his virtuous beauty masks a potential for vicious habits: "If some suspect of ill masked not thy show, / Then thou alone kingdoms of hearts shouldst owe." The poet calculatedly appeals to the youth's vanity in the hopes of encouraging upright behavior.

• **canker**   destructive worm.

SONNET 71

In this and the next three sonnets, the poet's mood becomes increasingly morbid. Here he anticipates his own death: "No longer mourn for me when I am dead / . . . / From this vile world, with vilest worms to dwell." The elegiac mood expresses a sense of loss as much for the poet's departed youth as for the actual prospect of death. Note that the poet characterizes the world as "vile," a strong condemnation of the age in which artificial beauty is more cherished than the young man's natural beauty.

The poet asks the young man not to grieve for him when he is dead, or even remember his name. Never wanting to cause the youth pain, the poet is afraid that, if the young man grieves for him, his woeful thoughts will replace any loving affection he may still have for the poet. Because the young man does not appear to be as infatuated with the poet as the poet is with the young man, such sentiment on the poet's part is rather presumptuous, especially when he then adds, "But let your love even with my life decay." Given the youth's slighting the poet earlier in the sonnets, at this point it would not be unreasonable to ask what "love" the poet thinks the youth still has for him.

In the final couplet, the poet urges the youth not to grieve for him "Lest the wise world should look into your moan / And mock you with me after I am gone." Again the poet is more concerned about the young man's reputation than he is about his own.

SONNET 72

Sonnet 72 echoes the mood of Sonnet 71, and the poet tells the youth not to praise his verse after the poet's death, as his praise could not add to the merit of the poems and may bring ridicule to the youth. The poet's self-denial displays a sense of hard-learned lessons: "My name be buried where my body is, / And live no more to shame nor me, nor you." Although the poet never questions his own love for the youth, he does question the worth of his sonnets, perhaps because they do not bring him the young man's affection. And yet he never gives up hope of pleasing his friend or of protecting him from criticism from others: "For I am shamed by that which I bring forth, / And so should you, to love things nothing worth." His characterizing his sonnets as "nothing worth" is one of the low points in the sonnets.

SONNET 73

The poet indicates his feeling that he has not long to live through the imagery of the wintry bough, twilight's afterglow, and a fire's dying embers. All the images in this sonnet suggest impending death. In the first quatrain, the poet compares himself to autumn leaves, but he is unable to pinpoint their exact number, just as he cannot determine how close he is to death: "When yellow leaves, or none, or few, do hang / Upon those boughs which shake against the cold." In the second quatrain, he talks of "twilight" as "after the sun fadeth in the west,"—a traditional metaphor for death. Death is close to the poet in this second quatrain, for he imagines death twice more, first as "black night" and then as sleep, "Death's second self." The third quatrain recalls Sonnet 45, in which the poet likened his desire for the young man to "purging fire." Now, however, his fire is but dying embers, a "deathbed" fueled by his love for the youth, "Consumed with that which it was nourished by."

Note the pause indicated by the period after each quatrain in the sonnet, the longest pause coming appropriately after the third quatrain, before the concluding couplet. The pauses after the first two quatrains are due to their beginning "In me thou seest. . . ." This phrase indicates that the poet is drawing an allusion between an external image and an internal state of mind, an association that in turn forces a slower reading of the lines, enabling some reflection on the emotional tone that each image evokes.

Now follows the couplet addressed to the youth that makes clear the conclusion to be drawn from the preceding lines: "This thou perceiv'st, which makes thy love more strong, / To love that well, which thou must leave ere long." Believing that he will soon die and never see the young man again, the poet's love for the youth intensifies.

SONNET 74

The poet continues his obsessive concern with his own death. Although he emphasizes his own inadequacy as a person, he boldly asserts the greatness of his verse: "My life hath in this line some interest, / Which for memorial still with thee shall stay." He claims that his better part will survive his death in his poems. In keeping with his exaggerated mood, the poet alludes to the belief that his demise will be "Too base" for the youth to remember, but the best part of him will survive in his immortal verse.

The poet's feeling that his sonnets are a memorial to the young man—and to the poet himself—is markedly different than his former attitude about his verse. Only two sonnets before, in Sonnet 72, he wrote of shame and characterized his verse as worthless: "For I am shamed by that which I bring forth, / And so should you, to love things nothing worth." But here in Sonnet 74, he claims that his verse has worth because it contains images of the youth, just as his body holds his soul. The concluding couplet, "The worth of that is that which it contains, / And that is this, and this with thee remains," restated means, "The human body has worth because it encapsulates the soul; these sonnets have worth because they encompass the youth's soul." The poet has come full circle—again—and now takes pride in his verse.

SONNET 75

The poet is torn by contrary feelings that he cannot reconcile. His relationship with the youth alternates between pleasure—"Sometime all full with feasting on your sight"—and uneasiness—"And by and by clean starved for a look." Nor does he know whether to be alone with his love or show it off to the world. Embedded in these words lurks a sense of dependence: "So are you to my thoughts as food to life, / Or as sweet-seasoned showers are to the ground." Following as it does the morbid sonnets dealing with death, in this sonnet the poet gains no pleasure either from fulfillment or desire: "Possessing or pursuing no delight / Save what is had or must from you be took."

SONNET 76

Complaining that his verse is sadly limited, the poet acknowledges that his praise of the young man allows no new form of argument. As a traditionalist, the poet rejects innovation for innovation's sake. Failing to keep abreast of modern inventions, he watches other poets experiment with new and exciting subjects and styles of writing: "Why, with the time, do I not glance aside / To new-found methods and to compounds strange?" He answers that, because his writing is all about the youth, and he can add nothing to the youth's beauty, it would do him no good to try newer styles because "all my best is dressing old words new, / Spending again what is already spent." The poet's verse is as recognizable as his name because, ultimately, his arguments are remarkably unvaried: "For as the sun is daily new and old, / So is my love still telling what is told."

SONNET 77

The youth's aging face will be reflected in a mirror, and the passage of time will be reflected on his watch, clashing with the youth's eternally young thoughts. As the young man ages, each wrinkle on his face will remind him of a memory from his youth. However, because the young man will not be able to remember every event from his life, the poet gives him a notebook in which to write his thoughts. This notebook, like the poet's sonnets, will become a history—a record of the young man's beauty while he was yet young.

SONNET 78

The poet's success in gaining entry into the youth's good graces inspires imitators: "As every alien pen hath got my use, / And under thee their poesy disperse." Acknowledging that he is being challenged by other poets for the young man's affections, the poet asks the youth to compare these imitators' verses against his own. Only then can the young man fully appreciate how wholly inspiring he is to the poet: "Yet be most proud of that which I compile, / Whose influence is thine, and born of thee." For others, the youth merely improves their style—"In others' works thou dost but mend the style"; for the poet, his young friend is "all my art"—subject, style, the reason for his writing the sonnets.

• **poesy**   poem.

SONNET 79

Sonnet 79 presents the first specific reference to a rival poet who vies for the young man's affections. Without losing his sense of moral superiority, the poet bitterly resents the other poet. His first response to the challenge is feeble and characteristically modest: "I grant, sweet love, thy lovely argument / Deserves the travail of a worthier pen." However, this modesty completely contradicts the sentiment of the next two lines: "Yet what of thee thy poet doth invent / He robs thee of, and pays it thee again." The rival poet boasts that he makes the young man beautiful in his verse, and yet, the poet argues, this rival cannot create the beauty that the poet has already discovered in the youth: The youth lends beauty to the verse, not the verse to the youth. Although the poet's anger at the rival poet is understated, five times in the sonnet he warns the young man of the rival poet's claiming to invent beauty in the young man's appearance.

SONNET 80

The poet acknowledges that the rival poet displaces him in the youth's favor. Feeling discouraged by the superiority of the "better spirit" of the rival poet, whom he describes throughout the sonnet using nautical imagery, the poet complains of being "tongue-tied," unable to compete with his rival's exalted verse.

The poet's phrasing is courteous, but the exaggerated language indicates a serious mood. One detects an ironic purpose in the poet's devotion in the face of rejection when he sarcastically compares his verse to the rival poet's as "My saucy bark, inferior far to his." He forgives his own abject behavior with the excuse that love for the young man is his sole reason for living and the sole reason for his destruction: "Then if he thrive, and I be cast away, / The worst was this: my love was my decay."

SONNET 81

The poet rebounds somewhat in the face of the rival poet's opposition. Reverting to tried-and-tested themes, he heroically assures the youth that he, unlike the rival poet, can immortalize the young man through his sonnets: "Your name from hence immortal life shall have, / Though I, once gone, to all the world must die." The poet's verse offers the young man a refuge from time's decay, but more importantly, it offers a haven to the poet himself during this crucial time when he is being challenged by the rival poet for the youth's affections. Although the curious contrast between the poet's humility about his person and his supreme confidence in his verse is still evident, he confidently asserts at the sonnet's end that the young man "still shall live" because "such virtue hath my pen."

SONNET 82

A less subdued poet challenges the rival poet. In contrast to the intellectually fashionable rival, the poet possesses an intuitive, almost spiritual inspiration. As wise as his rival is merely clever, he agrees with the young man that his verse may be inferior to the beauty of its subject, whose "worth" is greater than the poet's praise. The sonnet implies that the young man is too easily moved by the rival poet's flattery and will eventually tire of the "strained touches rhetoric can lend." But the poet's simple, unpretentious verse presents the youth in no false adornment, for the young man's beauty is more fanciful than any imaginative verse could ever be. Abhorring the "gross painting" that is in vogue with the rival poet and others like him, the poet emphasizes his own enduring ideals "In true plain words by thy true-telling friend"; in the final couplet, he foregoes his customary deference and courteous voice to register his indignation at his rival's exaggerated compliments, over which he is certain that his simple truths will prevail.

• **attaint** dishonor.

SONNET 83

Apparently having been reproached by the youth for withdrawing from competition against the rival poet, the poet argues that it is better not to write any poetry than to write falsely. Recalling the phrase "gross painting" from the previous sonnet, the poet responds to what must have been the young man's accusation, "I never saw that you did painting need, / And therefore to your fair no painting set"—as opposed to the rival poet, whose "modern quill doth come too short, / Speaking of worth, what worth in you doth grow." Apparently proud of the superiority of his verse, the poet scornfully contrasts his verse with the strained and rhetorical verse of his rival, who ironically minimizes the youth's beauty by his attempts to describe it: "For I impair not beauty, being mute, / When others would give life and bring a tomb." Setting his faith in his plain, sincere style, nonetheless the poet knows that the rival poet remains in the youth's favor: "There lives more life in one of your fair eyes / Than both your poets can in praise devise." He seems resigned to the rival poet's presence.

SONNET 84

The poet offers advice—while criticizing the rival poet—to any writer who wishes to achieve true poetry: Copying and interpreting nature are necessary for art, but lavishly ornamenting nature creates false art. For this reason, no distortion of the youth's beauty describes him. The poet need only tell the simple truth to flatter the youth best: "Let him but copy what in you is writ, / Not making worse what nature made so clear."

Criticizing the young man's addiction to praise as a mark of bad taste, the poet censures his friend for succumbing to the rival poet's glorification of him, which he says is merely prattle and therefore does the youth no good. The poet makes clear that the youth perpetuates the rival poet's false art: "You to your beauteous blessings add a curse, / Being fond on praise, which makes your praises worse." Clearly love does not distort the poet's judgment; his reproving the young man establishes his own independent spirit, which heretofore has been sadly lacking.

• **penury**   poverty.

SONNET 85

The poet likens himself to an "unlettered clerk" and finds his Muse "tongue-tied"—the identical phrase the poet used in Sonnet 80 to characterize himself. His rival seems a more gifted poet and a better-esteemed person, but in supposing himself and his work to possess little virtue, the poet maintains his usual ironic tone. The reader cannot, therefore, take his self-deprecating tone seriously, not so long as he continues to write the poetry that he says he despises: "I think good thoughts, whilst other write good words." Although he acknowledges that his own thoughts are expressed with greater refinement and grace by other poets, he maintains that his devotion to the young man has greater merit.

SONNET 86

Unlike the previous sonnets dealing with the rival poet, this last sonnet in the rival-poet sequence is written in the past tense and indicates that the rival is no longer a threat. Up to this point, the rival was shown gaining on the poet for the youth's affection, and the youth's encouragement of the rival poet deflated the poet's creative powers: "But when your countenance filled up his line, / Then lacked I matter; that enfeebled mine." The young man's inattention to the poet weakened the verse that the poet wrote during the youth's absence.

The image of the ship in the first two lines—"Was it the proud full sail of his great verse, / Bound for the prize of all-too-precious you"—makes clear the rival poet's real threat to the poet, but the poet argues—perhaps *too* staunchly, indicating more insecurity than he would have us believe—that at no time did his rival's poetic successes affect the poet's own verse: "No, neither he, nor his compeers by night / Giving him aid, my verse astonished." After completing a satirical portrait of his nemesis, the poet mocks the rival's pretensions—his solemnity, his bombast, and his delusions—and finally drops him from the sonnets' story line.

• **compeers by night**   spirit aids.

SONNET 87

Sonnet 87 reads like a conclusion to the sonnet sequence describing the dominance of the rival poet, but in fact is the poet's farewell to the youth, who has returned to him but "art too dear" for the poet to possess. The theme of farewell unifies this sonnet; in varying degrees, farewell is alluded to in the following nine poems. When the friendship between the poet and the young man collapses, only then does the poet discover that the young man was merely a "dream." He concedes defeat and bids the youth a regretful goodbye.

In the sonnet's first quatrain, the poet unequivocally bids farewell to the young man. Surprisingly, the tone is even-keeled rather than melodramatic, as if the poet were simply stating a fact and then explaining the reason for it: "Farewell: thou art too dear

for my possessing, / And like enough thou know'st thy estimate."
"Dear" in the first line implies that the youth is both too costly and
too much loved, and the legal terminology in the first four lines
suggests how flimsy is the poet's right to possess the youth.

The second and third quatrains explain further the poet's reasons for saying goodbye to the young man. In the second quatrain,
he characteristically reverts to questioning his own worth and
rhetorically asks why he ever thought he deserved the youth's affections: "And for that riches where is my deserving? / The cause of
this fair gift in me is wanting." The poet's eyes finally have been
opened about his relationship with the young man, for in the third
quatrain, he acknowledges that the strain in their friendship is the
fault of both: "Thyself thou gav'st, thy own worth then not knowing, / Or me, to whom thou gav'st it, else mistaking."

The final couplet leaves little doubt that the poet no longer de-
ludes himself about his and the young man's relationship.
Surveying his past actions, the poet concludes that only two av-
enues—fantasy and reality—were ever open for him: "Thus have I
had thee as a dream doth flatter, / In sleep a king, but waking no
such matter." Sadly, neither fantasy nor reality offers the poet any
consolation for the youth's emotional separation from him, for fantasy is make-believe, and reality exposes the gulf that exists—and
always existed—between himself and the youth.

- **patent** right.
- **misprision** error.

SONNET 88

The poet speaks of his relationship with the young man as
though it has been repaired after the rival poet's departure, but his
is a vision of how things *might* be rather than how they are. He pro-
poses to prove that the youth is virtuous—although the youth had
been disloyal—by insisting upon his own worthlessness and making their break appear the inevitable consequence of the poet's
faults: "Upon thy side against myself I'll fight / And prove thee virtuous, though thou art forsworn."

Defending against an injustice about to befall him, the poet allows that if the young man wants to humiliate him, then the poet will publicly and masochistically approve the disgrace: "Upon thy part I can set down a story / Of faults concealed wherein I am attainted, / That thou, in losing me, shall win much glory." At least there is none of the exaggerated modesty of previous sonnets. Although the poet remains at the youth's mercy emotionally, he deprives the youth of a clean rejection by agreeing to be dishonored. Ironically, in doing so, he achieves a unanimity of spirit—the very thing he wanted all along: "The injuries that to myself I do, / Doing thee vantage, double-vantage me." He characteristically falls into a state of emotional self-flagellation: "Such is my love, to thee I so belong, / That for thy right myself will bear all wrong."

SONNET 89

Continuing where the previous sonnet left off, this sonnet reveals an undertone of apprehension in the poet's references to the young man. Whatever the slanderous accusation the youth will make against him, the poet promises to prove the youth justified. Loving the young man and knowing that the young man wishes to forsake him will be enough to impel the poet to act against his own best interests.

So far the friendship is not completely dead. Throughout the sonnet, the poet uses the future tense because for all his insecurity and doubts, the dissolution of the relationship is not yet final. Hoping that such an end never occurs, the poet promises to correct any fault in himself that the youth might find. He consistently wars against himself for the youth's sake: "For thee, against myself I'll vow debate, / For I must ne'er love him whom thou dost hate." In other words, because the poet views himself and the youth as one indivisible person, if the youth should begin to hate the poet, then the poet would essentially begin to hate himself since he and the youth are the same person—at least in the poet's mind, but certainly not in the youth's.

• **haply**   by accident.

SONNET 90

Already distressed by "the spite of fortune," the poet urges the youth not to postpone his desertion of him if that is what he intends; do it at once, the poet begs: "Then hate me when thou wilt; if ever, now." His appeal for a swift and decisive action demonstrates how grave the crisis is to the poet. Phrases like "If thou wilt leave me" and "loss of thee," following upon "forsake me" in the preceding sonnet, indicate unmistakable anxiety, resentment, and grief felt by the poet. Afraid that everyone and everything are now against him, the poet fears most that the youth will "overthrow" him: "And other strains of woe, which now seem woe, / Compared with loss of thee will not seem so."

SONNET 91

The poet examines his love for the young man in a more relaxed, less urgent vein. He first catalogues different activities that people like to immerse themselves in, then he admits that he values the youth's precarious love more than any other sport or possession he already listed in the first quatrain; finally, he concludes of the young man, "And having thee, of all men's pride I boast." However, he remains doubtful about any joint future with his young love: "Wretched in this alone: that thou mayst take / All this away and me most wretched make." Coming as they do as the end couplet in the sonnet, these lines show just how vulnerable the poet is, for the word "wretched" appears twice in the couplet, and the complete stop after the alliterative phrase "me most wretched make" emphasizes the empty void that the poet is so fearful of when the youth finally abandons him.

SONNET 92

Resignedly, the poet is prepared to accept whatever fate brings. Because his life depends on the youth's love, his life will not survive the loss of that love and support: "And life no longer than thy love will stay, / For it depends upon that love of thine." Because even a much smaller injury than total rejection would emotionally affect him, why, the poet asks, should the youth inflict a far greater calamity by ending the relationship altogether? He is angry at the prospect of a capricious and summary rejection and, with open contempt of the young man's inconstant mind, declares that he will either be happy in the continued friendship or he will die. Ironically, his decision to die should the young man reject him causes him to doubt the young man's sincerity both now and in the past. Only here at the end of the relationship, with their continuing friendship questionable at best, is the poet willing to concede of the youth, "Thou mayst be false, and yet I know it not."

SONNET 93

In contrast to the concluding couplet in the previous sonnet, in which the poet questions the young man's moral character, now the poet surmises that the youth may be inconstant without knowing it. In this startling reversal, the poet acknowledges the essentially good nature of the youth, who is too beautiful to harbor evil impulses: "For there can live no hatred in thine eye." However, in the first quatrain, the poet asserts the strong possibility that he is being duped; no matter, he reasons, for the young man's beauty is more important than his moral character—a shallow and narcissistic assertion that the poet criticized the youth for believing in earlier sonnets.

All pretense is abandoned, and the poet accepts a certain amount of falseness in the relationship, living as the unsuspecting—yet knowing—victim of the youth's deceit. Because this hypocrisy affects only the youth's moral character but not his beauty, the poet will love him "Whate'er thy thoughts or thy heart's workings be." He acknowledges the risk he is taking in continuing to love the youth's appearance without being certain just how virtuous the young man is: "How like Eve's apple doth thy beauty grow / If thy sweet virtue answer not thy show!" Here, the poet is likening the young man to Eve's apple—a symbol of outward perfection but internal vice: The young man has a beautiful appearance, but he may be morally worm-eaten with vice.

SONNET 94

On the surface at least, Sonnet 94 continues the theme from the previous sonnet, which contrasts virtue with appearance. Although the sonnet offers a warm testimonial to a cool and impassive youth, there is no specific mention of the poet or the young man in the entire poem.

The "they" in the first line sums up the youth's characteristics: He is detached, impersonal, and authoritative. In the second quatrain, the "they" ironically pictures a youth who has a stingy, hoarding nature. The third quatrain, which seems at first to be disconnected from the first two, presents an image of a summer flower that is "to the summer sweet" but that succumbs easily to "base infection," meaning that in competition with more unsightly and noxious weeds, the summer flower will lose out. How this third quatrain is related to the first two is explained in the concluding couplet: "For sweetest things turn sourest by their deeds; / Lilies that fester smell far worse than weeds." Outward appearance does not necessarily correspond to an object's worth or character. The youth who in the first quatrain is detached and impersonal is really a tease; in the second quatrain, those persons who are "the lords and owners of their faces" are deceptive because they create false appearances; and finally, the summer flower may appear beautiful and vivacious, but it falters easily when faced with an obstacle such as "the basest weed." The entire sonnet, then, is an extended metaphor highlighting the dichotomy between outward appearance—mere show—and inner worth—an object's or person's true nature.

Much criticism has been written about Sonnet 94. According to one group of critics, Shakespeare advances the argument of those who, with an outward beauty that is the source of temptation, are themselves cold and not easily tempted. In contrast are those whose beauty not only tempts but also leads them into temptation. As a symbol of the first, the flower that is sweet to the world around it, although it blossoms and dies by itself, is self-contained. As a symbol of the second, the same flower is infected with a canker, in which case it is more offensive than a weed.

Other critics argue that Sonnet 94 is extremely ironic. Superior individuals remain aloof and never submit to temptation, but are not selfish in so doing, for they unconsciously do good deeds, like the flowers. The youth, the poet continues, must be, indeed already is, quite like these superior individuals—although just what this good is that the youth does certainly remains questionable. Yet even such superior individuals must remain alert not to fall from perfection if they are to avoid becoming the worst, just as "Lilies that fester smell far worse than weeds."

SONNET 95

Employing a paternal attitude, the poet continues his lecture on how deceiving appearances can be. In the first quatrain, he constructs a simile in which the young man is like a "fragrant rose" in which vice, likened to a destructive worm, grows unchecked. The poet doesn't condemn the young man but instead seems almost joyful that the youth's beauty hides such vice: "O, in what sweets dost thou thy sins enclose!" In the second quatrain, the poet criticizes himself for "making lascivious comments" about the youth's younger days, and we come to understand that the "shame" in line 1 is actually the "ill report" that the poet makes of the young man. But merely to mention the youth's name as the poet does turns malice into a compliment about him: "Naming thy name blesses an ill report." In the last quatrain, the poet again addresses the youth's ability to mask any vice in his character. This time, the poet likens the youth to a mansion "Where beauty's veil doth cover every blot / And all things turns to fair that eyes can see!" These lines' jubilant and almost proud tone is similar to that in the first quatrain.

Because the youth is utterly beautiful and the poet is entirely unappealing, they are ill-matched for union in a single being. The poet knows he can expect little pleasure from the relationship, yet he hesitates to make the final, complete break. Essentially he is the "shame / Which, like a canker in the fragrant rose, / Doth spot the beauty of [the youth's] budding name!" Knowing that the youth's behavior toward him is dishonorable because it is false, still the poet ingratiates himself to the young man. For example, in the final couplet, he calls him "dear heart," and his paternal affection for the youth prompts him to warn the young man, "The hardest knife ill used doth lose his edge." In other words, the beauty that the youth uses to cover his faults will ultimately fail him; the more he tries to compensate for his inner vices by maintaining his outer appearance, the faster that beautiful exterior will fail. Ultimately he will be exposed, not as an attractive man, but as a manipulating tease.

SONNET 96

Still using the paternal tone, the poet observes that the young man's vices are a subject of public gossip. The contrast between the youth's beauty and his vicious way of life makes the vices seem less immoral than otherwise: "Thou mak'st faults graces that to thee resort." The youth's ability to transform defects in his personality into attributes says more about his shallow society of friends and suitors, obviously more concerned with appearance than substance, than it does about the youth himself. How gullible must people be not to see through the young man's flimsy veneer, and how pathetic must the poet be to continue supporting the youth's reputation. The concluding couplet, which is identical to the last two lines in Sonnet 36, contradicts the "ill report" from the previous sonnet. Now the poet presents a "good report" of the youth. That these two lines are identical to the final couplet in Sonnet 36 demonstrates just how much the poet has regressed to his earlier dependence on the youth. Sadly, he has learned nothing over the course of some sixty sonnets. At this point, it appears that he is emotionally unable to bid the young man farewell.

SONNET 97

The poet begins a new sequence of sonnets, written in his absence from the youth during the summer and autumn months, although the first image in Sonnet 97 is of winter. The previous positions of the young man and the poet are now reversed, and it is the poet who apologizes for repudiating the relationship by associating with other friends.

Clearly a lapse in the poet's fortitude, as well as his judgment, is indicated since he wishes to renew the relationship that the youth callously dismissed. There is a nostalgic tone in the poet's reminiscence: "How like a winter hath my absence been / From thee, the pleasure of the fleeting year!" Images of different seasons, which are evoked principally for contrast, reflect such mood shifts, from gaiety to despair. For example, autumn is characterized as "teeming"—meaning bountiful—with "rich increase" of the harvest. But "teeming" also means "pregnant," so that although trees are bearing fruit, nevertheless the poet feels barren because he and the youth are separated. This archaic meaning of "teeming" as pregnant also explains the poet's use of the phrases "widowed wombs," "abundant issue," and "orphans and unfathered fruit"—all images connected with childbearing.

When the friend is away, then whatever the true season, it is like barren winter for the poet. Even summer becomes winter, "For summer and his pleasures wait on thee, / And, thou away, the very birds are mute." The image of winter, symbolizing both physical and emotional "freezings," unites the sonnet, which begins and ends with the poet lamenting being alone.

SONNET 98

The theme of absence continues with the youth away. The poet first describes April in a buoyant tone, and says that even "heavy Saturn," which during the Elizabethan period was thought to influence dark and gloomy behavior in people, "laughed and leapt" during this spring.

The typical reversal expected in the sonnets, either in the third quatrain or in the concluding couplet, appears early in Sonnet 98, coming at the beginning of the second quatrain with the word "Yet." That this change of fortune comes so early emphasizes just how despondent the poet is while separated from the young man. Neither birds nor flowers grant relief from his depressed emotional state, for he compares these spring and summer objects of beauty to the youth's beauty and concludes that they are imperfect copies of his friend's appearance: "They were but sweet, but figures of delight, / Drawn after you, you pattern of all those."

Recalling the previous sonnet, the poet again thinks of his separation from the young man as a barren winter. No longer critical of the youth, rather he becomes apologetic for the feeble nature of his verse, as though he is merely passing the time by writing frivolous sonnets while he is away from his beloved: "Yet seemed it winter still, and, you away, / As with your shadow I with these did play." The poet's use of the term "shadow" is similar to when he dreamt of the youth in earlier sonnets; this reference again demonstrates just how much the poet has regressed to his earlier, dependent attitude toward the youth.

SONNET 99

Sonnet 99 is an in-depth explanation of how the natural objects from lines 11 and 12 in the previous sonnet pale in comparison to the young man's beauty: "They were but sweet, but figures of delight, / Drawn after you, you pattern of all those." A charming artificiality in this sonnet illustrates the kind of lavish and elaborate praise the poet could write to win the youth's favor. Ironically, however, the sonnet also shows the poet's equivocal attitude in condemning such hyperbole: He practices what he criticizes.

Comprising fifteen lines instead of the usual fourteen, the sonnet seems an ingenious exercise in compliment rather than an expression of simple feeling. The first line—"The forward violet thus did I chide"—acts as a prelude, and the sonnet proper, composed of the next fourteen lines, describes exactly what this chiding entails. Wherever the poet looks in nature, he finds colors, smells, and shapes that mimic—and thereby steal from—the youth's beauty. Essentially he argues that the youth is the originating source from which nature draws its many hues and odors: "More flowers I noted, yet I none could see / But sweet or color it had stol'n from thee." The carefully wrought verse seems more an exercise in poetry-writing than it does an expression of genuine emotion.

SONNET 100

Sonnet 100 marks a change in the poet's thinking from previous sonnets, in which the simplicity of his poetry was expected to win favor against rivals, and suggests the poet's ebbing affection for the youth. We know that some time has elapsed since he wrote the previous sonnet because the poet rebukes himself for having neglected writing verse about the young man: "Where art thou, Muse, that thou forget'st so long / To speak of that which gives thee all thy might?" In an easy, relaxed tone, the poet exhorts himself to compose compliments about the youth, for now there is no rival

76

poet to curry the youth's attention: "Return, forgetful Muse, and straight redeem / In gentle numbers time so idly spent." Note the scythe and "crooked knife" references to death and time's decay in the concluding couplet; the poet seems unable—or unwilling—to create new images in his verse.

• **resty** lazy.

SONNET 101

Continuing his plea to the Muse of poetry, the poet abandons his silence and philosophizes about the nature of truth and beauty. Nature, he says, is the poet's truth; cosmetic beauty, his falsehood: "Truth needs no color with his color fixed, / Beauty no pencil, beauty's truth to lay." He also returns to another of his favorite themes, the young man's immortality through his verse; he recognizes that his only responsibility in life is "To make him much outlive a gilded tomb / And to be praised of ages yet to be."

SONNET 102

To justify not writing verse about the young man, the poet argues that constantly proclaiming love for someone cheapens the genuineness of the emotion. His tone is cautious because he detects a change in his feelings for the youth: "My love is strength-'ned, though more weak in seeming; / I love not less, though less the show appear." He recalls the formation of his relationship with the youth—rather than the current status of the friendship; this recollection is now the only inspiration for his writing and emphasizes just how far apart the two have grown. Because he expects the youth to be indifferent, he is firm but courteous when he refrains from writing verse: "I sometime hold my tongue, / Because I would not dull you with my song."

• **Philomel** the nightingale.

SONNET 103

The poet continues to bewail his abandonment by his Muse, although he concedes that his love for the youth is stronger because of the absence: "The argument all bare is of more worth / Than when it hath my added praise beside." In other words, the descriptions of love detract from the real emotion because the focus is more on the description of love than on love itself. He apologizes yet again that his verse is too poorly written to do justice to the young man's beauty.

SONNET 104

Sonnet 104 indicates for the first time that the poet and young man's relationship has gone on for three years. Evoking seasonal imagery from previous sonnets, the poet notes that "Three winters cold / . . . three summers' pride, / Three beauteous springs to yellow autumn turned / In process of the seasons I have seen." Only now is the poet willing to question whether the youth's beauty remains as it was "when first your eye I eyed": "So your sweet hue, which methinks still doth stand, / Hath motion, and mine eye may be deceived." No matter, though, the poet argues in the concluding couplet, if the youth's beauty has deteriorated: No beauty has ever equaled the youth's appearance, nor will anything in the future outshine his lovely visage.

SONNET 105

As if it weren't already clear, the poet writes that he has only one true love and that his poetry is only for the youth—the identical assertion presented in Sonnet 76. Just as the youth's beauty is immortal, so too is the poet's unchanging love for the youth: "Kind is my love to-day, to-morrow kind, / Still constant in a wondrous excellence."

Sonnet 105 repeats the contradictory idea that a "Fair, kind, and true" truth offers infinite scope for the poet's imagination. Only within the confines of a definite form does the imagination discover the meaning of infinity: "Fair, kind, and true have often lived alone, / Which three till now never kept seat in one"—in the young man. The youth's beauty is always the subject matter of the poet's verse, but there are infinite ways to express this beauty. However, whether the various means the poet employs truly express the youth's beauty is highly debatable.

SONNET 106

Sonnet 106 is addressed to the young man without reference to any particular event. The poet surveys historical time in order to compare the youth's beauty to that depicted in art created long ago. Not surprisingly, he argues that no beauty has ever surpassed his friend's. Admiring historical figures because they remind him of the youth's character, the poet contends that what earlier artists took for beauty was merely a foreshadowing of the youth's unsurpassed appearance: "So all their praises are but prophecies / Of this our time, all you prefiguring."

In the final couplet, the poet compares historical time with the present and finds that, although he has criticized his forerunners for their lack of definitive descriptions of beauty, he, too, is unable to describe adequately the young man's beauty. In lines 11 and 12, he surmises that earlier artisans never would have been able to do artistic justice to the young man: "And, for they looked but with divining eyes, / They had not still enough your worth to sing." However, he admits in the sonnet's last two lines that he doesn't have the necessary skills either: "For we, which now behold these present days, / Had eyes to wonder, but lack tongues to praise." Note the parallel imagery in the sonnet's last four lines, in which the past and the present are contrasted: "Eyes" are capable of viewing the youth's beauty, but previous artisans didn't have the skill "to sing" about the young man, and neither has the poet the skill "to praise" him adequately.

SONNET 107

Whereas the previous sonnet compared the past with the present, Sonnet 107 contrasts the present with the future. The poet's favorite theme of immortality through poetic verse dominates the sonnet.

In the first quatrain, the poet contends that his love for the young man is immortal. Although neither he nor "the prophetic soul" knows what the future holds, the poet maintains that only one thing is certain: his continuing affection for the youth, "Supposed as forfeit to a confined doom." The duration of the poet's love cannot be predicted. Nothing, he says, "Can yet the lease of my true love control." His love is not subject to time, nor controlled by uncertainty about the youth, nor by death itself.

In the second and third quatrains, the poet catalogues various images that emphasize endurance over change. These images parallel his immutable love for the youth, which he expands on when he claims that even death holds no sway over him and his sonnets: "I'll live in this poor rime, / While he insults o'er dull and speechless tribes." Other people—"tribes"—may succumb to time's decay but not the poet.

The final couplet speaks of the young man's deliverance from tyranny and death by means of the sonnets, a now-familiar theme of the poet's. Antithetical images of events, changing from peaceful, stable times to turmoil and civil strife, are of no concern to the poet, who asserts, as he does elsewhere, that the young man will triumph over all that the future has to offer: "And thou in this shalt find thy monument / When tyrants' crests and tombs of brass are spent." Poetry becomes prophecy.

- **augurs**   fortune tellers.

- **presage**   predict.

SONNET 108

Admitting that he risks running out of new ideas and "must each day say o'er the very same" about the young man, the poet replaces newly imagined creation with ritual; redundant love finds new meaning in repetition "So that eternal love in love's fresh case / Weighs not the dust and injury of age." Psychologically unhealthy, the poet again regresses to viewing himself and the young man as "thou mine, I thine." He relives the past, but he does so in such a way that the past seems newly fresh: "Finding the first conceit of love there bred / Where time and outward form would show it dead." Because reality entails past hurts and accusations, the poet chooses to live in a fantasy world where he's not forced to remember the youth's narcissistic treatment of him.

SONNET 109

Sonnet 109 begins a sequence of apologetic sonnets using the image of travel as a metaphor for the poet's reduction of the attention he gives to the young man. He defends his absence against charges of infidelity and indifference. Beneath his apologetic manner, one detects an assertion of independence from the youth's control: "O, never say that I was false of heart, / Though absence seemed my flame to qualify." In other words, although the poet's love for the youth never lessened, he would have been justified if it had.

Three times the poet declares that no matter where he may travel—both physically and in his thoughts—he will always return to the youth, for the young man is his alter ego. This theme of unity, which was a dominant theme in earlier sonnets, including the phrase "thou mine, I thine" from the previous sonnet, is expressed in the phrases "my soul, which in thy breast doth lie," "That is my home of love," and "thou art my all." However, these sentiments seem more like responses to criticism of the poet's having traveled away from the young man than they do sincere, impromptu declarations of affection.

SONNET 110

The poet deeply regrets his lapse of attention to the young man and wishes to show his disgust and self-reproach. He lists his faults and expresses resentment at being bound to his "motley" course and for selling "cheap what is most dear"—his love for the young man. Almost masochistically, he believes that he has hurt himself, a self-injury deserving the youth's reproach as well.

Sonnet 110 is unified by the poet's notion of truth and the many different ways truth is expressed: "'tis true," "Most true," "looked on truth," and "pure and most most loving." The sonnet incorporates the poet's movement from regret of an earlier behavior to his fawning over the young man. In the first quatrain, the poet admits that he offended the young man by his actions, although just what those actions were he doesn't say until in the second quatrain: He displayed affection for "another youth." However, this brief relationship has only strengthened his love for the young man, whom he calls "my best of love." Vowing never again to "grind / On newer proof, to try an older friend," the poet begs the young man, "Then give me welcome, next my heaven the best," and he ingratiates himself to the youth by calling him his "pure and most most loving breast." The double use of the word "most," although it seems falsely affected, emphasizes the deep emotion the poet has for the youth, "A god in love" to whom the poet is "confined."

SONNET 111

Sonnet 111 focuses particularly on the poet's laments about his misfortunes. He resents that circumstances have forced him to behave as he has because fortune provided so meanly for his birth and "did not better for my life provide / Than public means which public manners breeds." Other than an allusion to work, the poet's remarks are general and do not explicitly identify his profession. In any case, he differs from the young man in that he possesses no independent, private means of livelihood. The phrase "public means," therefore, may mean that he must seek patronage through "public manner"—for example, the pursuit of favor through flattering verse. It does not, as some critics argue, necessarily mean that the poet is an actor associated with stagecraft.

The remark "Thence comes it that my name receives a brand" expresses the poet's determination to make amends for the insincerity of his flattering eulogies and for his having briefly abandoned the young man. He apologizes for his materialist motives and twice asks the young man to "Pity me."

• **eisell** vinegar.

SONNET 112

The first two lines recall the "brand" and the "pity" that the poet discussed in the previous sonnet: "Your love and pity doth th' impression fill / Which vulgar scandal stamped upon my brow." Exactly what caused this "vulgar scandal" is unclear, although many critics surmise that the poet is a public performer who has received notoriety because of a past action, perhaps a bad performance onstage. The poet does not care what critics or flatterers think so long as the young man does not think ill of him: "For what care I who calls me well or ill, / So you o'er-green my bad, my good allow?" The creative term "o'er-green" is Shakespeare's own invention and refers to the poet's hopes the young man will conceal the "vulgar scandal" with his love.

As in earlier sonnets, the poet stresses the young man's importance to him. He continues to place great faith in the youth, who remains his only standard of measurement. "You are my all the world," he tells the youth, a sentiment that he emphasizes in the final couplet: "You are so strongly in my purpose bred / That all the world besides methinks are dead." It now appears that the poet's affections for "another youth" are truly dead, which he promised they were in Sonnet 110.

SONNET 113

More from a sense of duty than a meaningful expression of emotion, the poet professes to see the young man in everything while he is away from the youth. The eye-mind dichotomy presented in the first line—"Since I left you, mine eye is in my mind"— recalls earlier sonnets in which thoughts of the young man contented the poet during their separation. Additionally, the use of the words "most" and "true" in the rhyming couplet is similar to their use in Sonnet 110 and hints that the poet is still trying to prove—perhaps more to himself than to the young man—his re-energized love for the youth: "Incapable of more, replete with you, / My most true mind thus maketh mine eye untrue." Here, "most true mind" means that the only truth that the poet recognizes is his complete devotion to the young man.

SONNET 114

Continuing the dichotomy between the eye and the mind, the poet presents two alternative possibilities—indicated by the phrase "Or whether"—for how the eye and mind work. Either the mind controls the poet's seeing and is susceptible to flattery, or his eye is the master of his mind and makes "monsters and things indigest / Such cherubins" that resemble the youth. The poet decides on the first possibility, that his mind controls his sight; whatever the eye sees and whatever comparisons it makes, his mind transforms any object in the best light of the youth. The poet's eye "well knows" what is agreeing to the poet's mind "And to his [the mind's] palate doth prepare the cup."

Ironically, the poet acknowledges that comparing everything to the youth is unwise, for then he never truly judges either the youth or the world. However, he accepts the risk, for in the sonnet's final two lines he says that even if his mind is deceiving itself, at least the beautiful appearance of the youth is consolation for this self-deception. In other words, the poet does not care if something is poisoned so long as it is beautiful; appearance is more important than substance.

SONNET 115

The poet now admits that his believing that his love for the youth was as great as it could ever be was wrong: He can love the young man even more fully than he has done in the past. Comparing how things change over time to his newfound knowledge of how much his love for the youth can yet increase, the poet questions why he let time scare him into previously saying "Now I love you best" to the youth when his love for the young man grows the longer the poet knows him.

Although the poet now realizes that his love for the youth may increase even more, there is also a sense that the poet gets what he *deserves* rather than what he *wants*. His past confidence in how much he loved the youth was false, which is why he cannot say "Now I love you best": "Alas, why, fearing of Time's tyranny, /

Might I not then say, 'Now I love you best' / . . . / . . . doubting of the rest?" And yet such security is exactly what the poet craves. He wants to say decisively that at the current time he loves the youth as much as he can ever love him, but "Love is a babe; then might I not say so, / To give full growth to that which still doth grow." The poet's again saying that now is the time that he most loves the youth may be detrimental, for such an expression may very well limit any future growth in the relationship.

SONNET 116

Despite the confessional tone in this sonnet, there is no direct reference to the youth. The general context, however, makes it clear that the poet's temporary alienation refers to the youth's inconstancy and betrayal, not the poet's, although coming as it does on the heels of the previous sonnet, the poet may be trying to convince himself again that "Now" he loves the youth "best." Sonnet 116, then, seems a meditative attempt to define love, independent of reciprocity, fidelity, and eternal beauty: "Love's not Time's fool, though rosy lips and cheeks / Within his bending sickle's compass come." After all his uncertainties and apologies, Sonnet 116 leaves little doubt that the poet is in love with love.

The essence of love and friendship for the poet, apparently, is reciprocity, or mutuality. In Sonnet 116, for example, the ideal relationship is referred to as "the marriage of true minds," a union that can be realized by the dedicated and faithful: "Let me not to the marriage of true minds / Admit impediments." The marriage service in the Episcopal *Book of Common Prayer*—"If any of you know cause or just impediment"—provides the model for the sonnet's opening lines. In them, we see the poet's attitude toward love, which he proceeds to define first negatively. He explains what love is not, and then he positively defines what it is. The "ever-fixed mark" is the traditional sea mark and guide for mariners—the North Star—whose value is inestimable although its altitude—its "height"—has been determined. Unlike physical beauty, the star is not subject to the ravages of time; nor is true love, which is *not* "Time's fool."

The poet then introduces the concepts of space and time, applying them to his ideal of true love: "Love alters not with his brief hours and weeks, / But bears it out even to the edge of doom." Note that the verb "alters" is lifted directly from line 3, in which the poet describes what love is not. "Bears it out" means survive; "edge of doom," Judgment Day. Finally, with absolute conviction, the poet challenges others to find him wrong in his definition: "If this be error and upon me proved, / I never writ, nor no man ever loved." Just how secure the poet is in his standards of friendship and love, which he hopes that he and the youth can achieve, is evident in this concluding couplet; he stakes his own poetry as his wager that love is all he has described it to be.

SONNET 117

The poet abruptly returns to the subject of the young man and renews his apology and appeal. Whereas Sonnet 116 indicates that the relationship has stabilized, this sonnet stresses the poet's self-rebuke using legal terminology: "Accuse me thus, that I have scanted all / Wherein I should your great deserts repay"; ". . . all bonds do tie me day by day"; and "Book both my wilfulness and errors down."

Sonnet 117 echoes Sonnet 110, in which the speaker also lists his faults. Here, although the octet—the first eight lines—clearly renders the nature of the poet's wrongs, actual events are not identified. The poet confesses to squandering the youth's constant affection on others: "I have frequent been with unknown minds." The figurative expression "hoisted sail to all the winds" may refer to emotional distance or, as some think, to excessive drink rather than actual travel. The ending couplet again makes clear, as in the previous sonnet, that the emotional gulf between the youth and the poet is due to the youth's inconstancy and betrayal, not the poet's.

• **scanted**   be short of.

86

SONNET 118

The poet now elaborates on lines 5 and 6 from the previous sonnet: "That I have frequent been with unknown minds / And given to time your own dear-purchased right." Here in Sonnet 118, because a jaded appetite needs reviving, both the poet and the youth seek new, if not better, acquaintances. When the poet compares the youth to a "ne'er-cloying sweetness," he sets up an antithesis in describing his newer friends as "eager compounds" and "bitter sauces." Declaring himself to be "diseased," the poet is displeased in his choice of medicines: "To bitter sauces did I frame my feeding." Reacting to the youth's emotional withdrawal from the relationship, the poet overreacts and finds that the cure to his ailing heart is worse than the original malady of unrequited love. Where originally there was no sickness, now there are "faults assured," but only after the fact does the poet realize his mistake: "But thence I learn, and find the lesson true, / Drugs poison him that so fell sick of you." Mutual affection between the poet and the youth is in decline.

• **meetness** fitness to the occasion.

SONNET 119

Arguing that his actions were impulsive and uncontrollable, the poet sincerely apologizes for betraying the youth. He describes the destruction of the relationship as tragic, for it is his most prized possession: "What wretched errors hath my heart committed, / Whilst it hath thought itself so blessèd never!" However, he acknowledges that there are some benefits from the relationship's demise. Sonnet 119 takes the reader from the poet's infatuation for the youth to his newfound attraction—the Dark Lady. Although she is never directly named, she is likened to "this madding fever," and hers are "Siren tears / Distilled from limbecks foul as hell within." Full of remorse, the poet returns to his old love with greater poignancy and ardor (lines 12 and 13). Nevertheless, there is more hope than certainty that by "ruined love" rebuilt he shall find a love made stronger by the breach.

• **limbecks** gourd-shaped vessels used in distilling.

SONNET 120

The poet and the youth now are able to appreciate traded injuries, with the poet neglecting the youth for his mistress and the youth committing a vague "trespass." But their positions are only reversed in a rhetorical sense, for the poet still argues that they remain friends: "But that your trespass now becomes a fee; / Mine ransoms yours, and yours must ransom me." Sonnet 120 embodies yet another variation on the poet's transference of roles from sufferer—"And for that sorrow which I then did feel"—to inconstant wrongdoer—". . . you were by my unkindness shaken"—to tyrant—"And I, a tyrant, have no leisure taken." The poetic story suddenly becomes complex and tortured by another's presence, although this presence remains in the background.

SONNET 121

The poet receives the same public reproof as the youth did earlier in the sonnets and is forced to consider whether or not his actions are immoral. Maintaining that "'Tis better to be vile than vile esteemed / When not to be receives reproach of being," under no circumstance will he tolerate hypocrisy. He will not defend the indefensible in himself but will admit the truth of his errors: "No, I am that I am; and they that level / At my abuses reckon up their own." The phrase "I am that I am" is biblical in its affirmation of self-knowledge and humility. The poet will not submit to the judgment of those with "false adulterate eyes" nor let them make evil what he holds to be good—although in the concluding couplet there is a hint of pessimism on the poet's part.

SONNET 122

Just as the poet gave a notebook to the youth in Sonnet 77, the youth has given the poet a notebook, which the poet discards. The poet, who knows more about the youth than any book can contain, says that he does not need a reminder of the young man. Rejecting the notebook is a curious gesture, almost uncaring, indicating how casual the relationship has become. Although the last two lines—"To keep an adjunct [aid] to remember thee / Were to import forgetfulness in me"—emphasize that the poet does not fear losing his memory of the youth, the entire sonnet implies that the youth is fast becoming only a dear memory to the poet, if he is not one already.

SONNET 123

The poet clearly denies that he is one of time's fools, or one who acts only for immediate satisfaction: "No, Time, thou shalt not boast that I do change." This theme of constancy is evident throughout the sonnet. After defiantly stating that he will not be duped into ending his love for the youth, the poet then philosophizes about how people perceive objects and events according to what they *want* to see, not what really is. The poet argues that because we live for only a brief span of time we value most what is old—that which has withstood the ravages of time and has existed much longer than any individual person—for example, the "pyramids" in line 2, which symbolize time's accumulation.

In the first two lines of the third quatrain, the poet again boldly asserts that his love is unlike these created images he just discussed: "Thy registers and thee I both defy, / Not wond'ring at the present nor the past." He then follows this assertion with an even greater boast in the concluding couplet: The one thing not affected by fortune or accident is the true vow of love. His brash statement "I will be true, despite thy scythe and thee" nicely balances the sonnet's opening line; his boast here at the sonnet's end counters time's boast at the sonnet's beginning.

SONNET 124

Developing further the theme of constancy from the previous sonnet, the poet argues that love—"that heretic"—is not subject to cancellation or change. Unlike other people's love, which is "subject to Time's love or to Time's hate," his constant love is not susceptible to injurious time: "No, it was builded far from accident; /

It suffers not in smiling pomp, nor falls / Under the blow of thrallèd discontent."

This obscure sonnet is fraught with political and religious references. The poet hypothetically calls his love "the child of state" but rejects this assertion in the concluding couplet, in which he castigates those people—"the fools of Time"—who "die for goodness, who have lived for crime"—that is, people who repent at the last moment of their lives. The figure of speech "fools of Time" also alludes to the poet's rivals, who pursue material reward, patronage, and self-interest in the name of love.

- **thrallèd**   oppressed.

SONNET 125

For the poet, love is not a matter of external pride—that is, he is not interested in his rivals' self-frustrating displays of false love (lines 1–2). The language here is philosophical, and the first quatrain suggests that the poet's public homage to the youth means little to the poet. The second quatrain reflects on the rivals who hope to win the youth's favor by sacrificing their imaginative resources on vain hopes. Playing off the image of tenants dwelling in their apartments and paying too much rent, the poet argues that his rivals for the youth's affection are "pitiful thrivers"—achievers of "form and favor" rather than of any real substance. In the third quatrain, the poet's offering to the youth is neither "mixed with seconds" nor "knows no art"; his affection for the youth is pure love, not like the artificial posturing of his rivals.

- **extern**   exterior.
- **oblation**   offering.

SONNET 126

Sonnet 126 is the last of the poems about the youth, and it sums up the dominant theme: Time destroys both beauty and love. However, the poet suggests that the youth, "Who hast by waning grown and therein show'st / Thy lovers withering as thy sweet self grow'st," remains beautiful despite having grown older. Because the youth is mortal, he will eventually die, but the poet does not appear to be as concerned with this future event as he was in earlier sonnets. Nor does the poet feel the need to state that the youth will live forever in the poet's sonnets. He is much more confident that his sonnets will exist forever—and the youth in them—and so does not feel it necessary to bring this to the youth's attention.

Unlike the previous sonnets, this sonnet consists of twelve lines in rhymed couplets, and it serves as the *envoi*—a short, closing stanza—of the sonnet sequence dealing with the young man. Now the poet is concerned with the ebb and flow of things, of renewal and degeneration. With this sonnet, the poet comes full circle from the deferential submission in the early sonnets to equality and independence, "poor but free." That is, he will no longer need to be tactful or guarded in his criticisms of the young man.

SONNET 127

Sonnet 127, which begins the sequence dealing with the poet's relationship to his mistress, the Dark Lady, defends the poet's unfashionable taste in brunettes. In Elizabethan days, so the poet tells us, black was not considered beautiful: "In the old age black was not counted fair, / Or, if it were, it bore not beauty's name." However, what is considered beautiful—at least to the poet—has changed; "now is black beauty's successive heir." This change in what is considered beautiful is the poet's main concern here in Sonnet 127 and in succeeding sonnets.

What most upsets the poet is not that one definition of beauty supersedes another but that women use cosmetics to enhance their natural appearance. This unnatural practice creates artificiality, "Fairing the foul with art's false borrowed face." Even worse, cosmetics devalue the ideal, or standard, of what beauty is, for they allow women to change their appearances on a whim according to what is currently deemed beautiful. Constancy in what is beautiful is sacrificed for fickle, mercurial notions of how a woman should look: "Sweet beauty hath no name, no holy bower, / But is profaned, if not lives in disgrace."

The degree of emphasis on the Dark Lady's color varies in the sonnets, so sometimes she seems black-haired and other times merely brunette. The poet's appreciation of the Dark Lady's appearance is complex: He is glad that she does not use cosmetics to lighten her appearance, which would be "a bastard shame," but she is not physically attractive to the poet, for all her erotic appeal. However, her black eyes become her so well "That every tongue says beauty should look so." Black, then, becomes another means for the poet to discredit the use of cosmetics; his mistress' good looks are not "slandered" by unnatural measures.

SONNET 128

Sonnet 128 is one of the few sonnets that create a physical scene, although that scene involves only the poet standing beside "that blessed wood"—probably a harpsichord, a stringed instrument resembling a grand piano—that the Dark Lady is playing. The sonnet is comparable to Sonnet 8 in that both concern music, but Sonnet 128 speaks of "my music" while Sonnet 8 speaks of "Music to hear," a subtle distinction in feeling, with Sonnet 128 the more sensual of the two.

Jealous of his mistress' touching the instrument rather than him, the poet fantasizes about kissing the woman in the same tender, controlling manner that she uses when playing. What makes the sonnet so physically sensual despite the poet's never once touching the woman is not only his description of her playing technique but his personification of the instrument's response to the woman's touch. He envies "those jacks that nimble leap / To kiss the tender inward of [the woman's] hand" and resents "those dancing chips, / O'er whom [the woman's] fingers walk with gentle gait"; in his mind, his "poor lips" should be kissing her, not she the "dead wood."

In the concluding couplet, the poet continues to personify the wooden instrument's levers, calling them "saucy jacks so happy" because the woman physically touches them. The only consolation the poet has is his fantasy of kissing his mistress, which is an empty comfort given that the poet craves the sensuous touch the Dark Lady uses as she plays the musical instrument.

SONNET 129

The mistress is not mentioned in this sonnet. Instead, the poet pens a violent diatribe against the sin of lust. The sonnet's angry attack on sexual pleasure stands between two rather innocuous sonnets addressed to the woman at the keyboard, and serves as a commentary on the morning following a night of pleasurable indulgences. The poet suffers a kind of panic in realizing how vulnerable he is to losing self-control to lascivious impulses. It is the paradox of having to fully let go in order to enjoy emotional release yet regretting the inescapable loss of control, the same control he was jealous of the mistress having over the "dead wood."

Although Sonnet 129 never directly refers to any character, it does indirectly express the poet's character in strongly marked antithesis, the excited impatience of lust contrasted with the revulsion that follows gratification:—"A bliss in proof and proved, a very woe; / Before, a joy proposed; behind, a dream." The poet often reverses the order of words to give greater impact to his antithesis and to deepen the impression of conflict, as in line 2: "Is lust in action; and till action, lust." Line 14—"To shun the heaven that leads men to this hell"—completes the antagonistic imagery.

Sonnet 129 reveals a fundamental weakness in the poet's moral being. He asks why his heart should be moved by what he knows to be worthless, and yet, obviously bound by passion, he cannot escape his lust despite his better self. He endeavors to convince himself that the Dark Lady is better than he knows her to be.

SONNET 130

Sonnet 130 is a parody of the Dark Lady, who falls too obviously short of fashionable beauty to be extolled in print. The poet, openly contemptuous of his weakness for the woman, expresses his infatuation for her in negative comparisons. For example, comparing her to natural objects, he notes that her eyes are "nothing like the sun," and the colors of her lips and breasts dull when compared to the red of coral and the whiteness of snow.

Whereas conventional love sonnets by other poets make their women into goddesses, in Sonnet 130 the poet is merely amused by his own attempt to deify his dark mistress. Cynically he states, "I grant I never saw a goddess go; / My mistress, when she walks, treads on the ground." We learn that her hair is black, but note the derogatory way the poet describes it: "black wires grow on her head." Also, his comment "And in some perfumes is there more delight / Than in the breath that from my mistress reeks" borders on crassness, no matter how satirical he is trying to be. The poet must be very secure in his love for his mistress—and hers for him—for him to be as disparaging as he is, even in jest—a security he did not enjoy with the young man. Although the turn "And yet" in the concluding couplet signals the negation of all the disparaging comments the poet has made about the Dark Lady, the sonnet's last two lines arguably do not erase the horrendous comparisons in the three quatrains.

• **dun**   tan or mud-colored.

SONNET 131

The poet further discusses his mistress's unattractive appearance. The first quatrain continues the previous sonnet's ending thought, that the Dark Lady is "the fairest and most precious jewel." However, after these opening four lines, the poet then acknowledges that to other people the Dark Lady's appearance is anything but lovely. Surprisingly, after the first quatrain, in which the poet speaks most assuredly about his love for his mistress, now he is unwilling to defend her publicly against slanderous remarks about her appearance. Speaking of those persons who hold that the Dark Lady "hath not the power to make love groan," the poet shies away from supporting her: "To say they [libelers] err I dare not be so bold, / Although I swear it to myself alone." He appears satisfied that his loving her privately is more important than what anyone else might think: "Thy black is fairest in my judgment's place." As the sonnet's last two lines make clear, to him only her deeds are black, in the sense of darkly malevolent. Despite his awareness of her low moral character, the poet remains infatuated with her. Line 14 shows his unwillingness to criticize her moral faults.

SONNET 132

Sonnet 132 represents an intensification of the poet's feelings for the Dark Lady, ironically paralleling his former relationship with the youth in that the poet recognizes that she does not love him. Built around an image of the woman's eyes, the sonnet is most notable for an extended pun on the words "morning" and "mourning."

The first quatrain leaves little doubt that the woman has no amorous feelings for the poet. Addressing the woman, the poet acknowledges that her heart "torments" him "with disdain." How does he know this? He sees her disaffection in her eyes, which "Have put on black and loving mourners be, / Looking with pretty ruth upon [his] pain." The word "mourners" in line 3 is punned in the first line of the second quatrain, in which the poet describes the woman's eyes in comparison to how the "morning sun of heaven / Better becomes the grey cheeks of the east." However, note how unflattering are the poet's comparisons between the woman's eyes and nature: Nature is not brightly shining; rather it is "grey" and "sober." The third quatrain completes the poet's thoughts in the second quatrain. The comparisons he makes are to the woman's "two mourning eyes" because of the pity she feels for him. Ironically, the woman's dark, "mourning" eyes make her even more attractive to the poet, who, in the concluding couplet, again swears allegiance to the woman's beauty and calls "foul" all other women whose looks are not as black as the Dark Lady's.

- **ruth** pity.

SONNET 133

Whereas Sonnet 132 makes the mistress into a chaste beauty, Sonnet 133 maligns her for seducing the poet's friend, the young man: "Beshrew that heart that makes my heart to groan / For that deep wound it gives my friend and me." Whether or not this "deep wound" is caused by the woman's having had a sexual affair with the youth is unclear. The "slave to slavery" phrase in line 4 may be more about jealousy than about lust, for the poet seems enamored here with both the woman and the young man.

The woman's pitiful eyes contrast with her cruel and flirtatious heart. Cynically, the "mourning eyes" of Sonnet 132 have become "cruel" eyes that torment the poet. Attempting to protect the youth from the woman's advances, the poet argues that because the young man resides in the poet's own heart, the woman can have the young man only by having the poet, whose heart will guard the heart of the youth from any cruelty the woman may do him. However, the sonnet's last two lines make clear that the poet knows that the woman will be cruel not only to him but to the young man.

• **beshrew**   a mild curse.

SONNET 134

The story of the poet's friend's seduction unfolds in Sonnet 134. Hoping to gain the woman's favor, the poet sends the young man to the woman with a message. However, she seizes the opportunity to make the youth her lover, and the youth responds to her advances wholeheartedly, as lines 7 and 8 suggest: "He learned but surety-like to write for me / Under that bond that him as fast doth bind." When the poet learns of the youth's entanglement, he blames himself, for the woman used him to entice the young man; now both he and the youth are involved with the mistress. For the poet, innocence and naivete explain the youth's behavior, but he fears that he has lost both the youth and his mistress.

Constructed around the image of usury (lending money at a high rate of interest), Sonnet 134 has a number of bawdy expressions. For example, line 2 introduces a pun on the word "will," which, in Elizabethan times, meant lust, desire, and either the male or the female sex organs. The sonnet is saturated with terms common to usury: The poet is "mortgaged" (used as security) by the woman (the "usurer") to gain the affections of the youth (the "debtor").

SONNET 135

The punning on the word "will" continues from the previous sonnet. The poet wants to continue his sexual relationship with his mistress, but she is already bursting with lovers: "Whoever hath her wish, thou hath thy Will, / And Will to boot, and Will in overplus." Here in just the first two lines, the word *Will* appears three times, but just who or what these *Wills* are remains ambiguous. One possibility is that each *Will* corresponds to the youth, the Dark Lady's husband, and even Shakespeare himself. Another possibility is that *Will* is a general term for lover; after all, one meaning of the word "will" during Elizabethan times was the male sex organ. Yet another, less bawdy possibility, is that the word *Will* refers to the weak personalities of her lovers, who are unable to decide their own fates because of the woman's strong, sexually magnetic personality; basically she controls them, and they have no free will to make decisions.

Because the woman already has several *Wills*, or lovers, the poet wonders why she does not accept him, his "will," as well: "So thou, being rich in Will, add to thy Will / One will of mine to make thy large Will more." Employing the image of the sea as a simile of the woman, the poet argues that the sea adds water to itself without exertion; so should the Dark Lady.

There is more than a little cynicism in the poet's admission of lust for a thoroughly disreputable woman. Begging to have sex with the woman, the poet barely masks his jealousy of the woman's many lovers: "Shall will in others seem right gracious, / And in my will no fair acceptance shine?" What is so wrong, he asks her, with his sex organ that she won't accept him as her lover? Sarcastically, he bawdily asks her why her own sex organ, which so easily accommodated other men's, cannot accept one more.

SONNET 136

Sonnet 136 continues to play on the word "will," and the result is still more damaging to the woman's character. The lady has other lovers but has not yet consented to accept the poet. In the last line, the poet acknowledges, "And then thou lovest me, for my name is Will," most likely a reference to Shakespeare himself.

For all of the poet's play on phrases like "I come so near," "store's account," and "a something, sweet," his satirical purpose is apparent. Essentially the poet's argument is that one more lover—

himself—will not overextend the mistress, especially when the poet characterizes himself as "nothing": "For nothing hold me, so it please thee hold / That nothing me, a something, sweet, to thee." The poet argues that, given the woman's prodigious lust, adding one more lover to her stable of lovers is insignificant.

SONNET 137

The dichotomy between the impulses of the eye and the heart is developed further in this sonnet. After the preceding two sexually comic sonnets, Sonnet 137 presents the poet seriously musing over just how false love can be. He first addresses Love, which he calls "A blind fool" and blames Love for misleading him about the woman's moral character. In the second quatrain, the poet asks Love why it encourages him to love the woman, "Whereto the judgment of [the poet's] heart is tied." Angry at, and highly uncomplimentary of the woman, the poet characterizes her as a loose woman, "the wide world's common place." Still the poet is confused, for he finds himself insensibly drawn to a woman whom he ought—in a more rational state of mind—to repudiate. The conflict between passion and judgment shows just how mortified and perplexed he is by his submission to an irrational, impulsive element of his personality: "Or mine eyes seeing this [the woman's wantonness], say this is not, / To put fair truth upon so foul a face." The mistress no longer is the focus of the sonnet; now the poet's concern is with the nature and workings of human judgment.

SONNET 138

Sonnet 138 presents a candid psychological study of the mistress that reveals many of her hypocrisies. Certainly she is still very much the poet's mistress, but the poet is under no illusions about her character: "When my love swears that she is made of truth, / I do believe her, though I know she lies." He accepts without protest her "false-speaking tongue" and expects nothing better of her. Cynically, he too deceives and is comforted by knowing that he is no longer fooled by the woman's charade of fidelity to him, nor she by how young and simpleminded he presents himself to be.

In a relationship without affection or trust, the two lovers agree to a relationship based on mutual deception. Both agree never to voice the truth about just how much their relationship is built on never-spoken truths: "But wherefore says she not she is unjust? / And wherefore say not I that I am old?" Note that the sentence construction in these two lines is identical, similar to how both the poet and the woman identically feign lying when each knows that the other person knows the truth.

The main theme of the concluding two lines is lust, but it is treated with a wry humor. The poet is content to support the woman's lies because he is flattered that she thinks him young—even though he knows that she is well aware of just how old he is. On the other hand, he does not challenge her pledges of faithfulness—even though she knows that he is aware of her infidelity. Neither is disposed to unveil the other's defects. Ultimately the poet and the woman remain together for two reasons, the first being their sexual relationship, the second that they are obviously comfortable with each other's lying. Both of these reasons are indicated by the pun on the word "lie," meaning either "to have sex with" or "to deceive": "Therefore I lie with her and she with me, / And in our faults by lies we flattered be."

SONNET 139

Regressing to his former melodramatic verse, the poet begs the woman to be honest with him and confess her infidelity. Coming as it does directly after the previous sonnet, in which the poet appears to have mastered his insecurities, the poet's sense of abandonment in Sonnet 139 is surprising. However, recalling his apparent helplessness in standing up to the young man's transgressions in earlier sonnets, the poet's response to the woman's continuing infidelity is expected.

Although weary of making excuses for the woman's wantonness, the poet's rationalizations persist. As long as the woman gives the poet her full attention when they are together, he will excuse her actions when they are apart: "Tell me thou lov'st elsewhere; but in my sight, / Dear heart, forbear to glance thine eye aside."

Plainly the poet still loves her; however, she humiliates him with her open flirtations. As with the youth, the poet allows the woman to dictate the terms of the relationship. Note the many phrases in which he begs the woman to act because he is unable to: "Wound me," "Use power with power and slay me," "Let me excuse thee," "Kill me," and "rid my pain." Unable to act resolutely, the poet begs the woman to dispatch him swiftly.

SONNET 140

Sinking quickly into despair over the sad state of his relationship with the woman, the poet threatens the woman with public humiliation should she not at least feign love for him. The first warning is in the first quatrain, in which he cautions her not to be too public in her flirtations with other men. In the second quatrain, the poet uses a simile to convey his thoughts of how the woman should treat him. Like a dying man who wants only false reassurances from his doctor about his condition, he wants the woman to falsify her love for the poet. Sadly, the poet's suggesting this action shows how knowledgeable he is that the relationship's end is near. The third quatrain contains another threat that the poet will publicly slander the woman's character: "For if I should despair, I should grow mad, / And in my madness might speak ill of thee." Lest the woman not heed his first two warnings, he adds a third in the sonnet's last three lines, overtly forewarning his mistress that "Slanderers by mad ears believed be," and that she should "Bear thine eyes straight, though thy proud heart go wide." In other words, when they are in public, she must pay attention only to him and not to any other man; if she does not do as he wishes, he will publicly slander her.

SONNET 141

In Sonnet 141, the poet discusses how his senses warn him of the woman's disreputable character, yet his heart, a symbol of his emotions, remains affectionately attached to her. He begins the sonnet by denying that the woman has any attractive features. His eyes note "a thousand errors" both in her appearance and her personality, but diametrically opposed to his eyes is his heart, which "despite of view is pleased to dote." All of his senses come into play in the second quatrain, in which he categorizes his repugnance for the woman. Stylistically, the first three lines in this second stanza begin identically with the word "Nor," followed by each of his senses: hearing ("Nor are mine ears "); touch ("Nor tender feeling"); and taste and smell ("Nor taste, nor smell"). The crux of his argument comes in the third quatrain and best sums up the dichotomy between his senses and his heart: "But my five wits nor my five senses can / Dissuade one foolish heart from serving thee." Neither mind nor his body can prevent him from loving her, but he is consoled by the pain she inflicts on him. Masochistically, he regards her cruel behavior as punishment for his sinful behavior: "That she makes me sin awards me pain." The word "sin" here means his outrageous rejection of common sense in loving her.

SONNET 142

Delving into the awareness of sin, Sonnet 142 sums up the poet's whole fatuous and insatiable passion. He supports the woman's rejection of his love because he deems his love for her unworthy of him: "Love is my sin and thy dear virtue hate, / Hate of my sin, grounded on sinful loving." He cannot help loving her, but he despises himself for doing so. Note that in lines 1 and 2, the poet compares himself to the woman using opposite qualities: The poet's "Love" opposes the woman's "hate," and "my sin" contrasts to the cynical "thy dear virtue." He believes that he deserves her contempt because of *her* damnable behavior, not because of *his*. Yet the poet feels that he deserves the woman's pity because he shares her vice. Hurt by her rejection of him, the satirical thrust of his argument is unmistakable: "Be it lawful I love thee as thou lov'st those / Whom thine eyes woo as mine importune thee." That is, he loves the woman in the same manner that she loves her many suitors: artificially, meanly, and basely. Ironically, however, her flirting with others becomes such an artful and "sinful loving" that he admires her and wants her more.

SONNET 143

The image of an errant mistress chasing chickens while neglecting her infant suggests a love triangle between the woman, the young man, and the poet. The youth is "one of her feathered creatures" and the poet "her babe." Incredibly, and almost pitifully, the poet again begs the woman to love him; he seems to have regressed to a baby needing its mother for shelter and support. To add insult to the poet's injury, he learns that the youth has tried to avoid the woman, but *she* pursues the youth: "But if thou catch thy hope [the youth], turn back to me / And play the mother's part, kiss me, be kind." So long as the woman sexually favors the poet, he will disregard her pursuit of the young man, which is the same argument that the poet makes in Sonnets 135 and 136. However, here in Sonnet 143, he states his request unequivocally, mincing no words about what he wants and how far he is willing to go to get it: "So will I pray that thou mayst have thy Will, / If thou turn back and my loud crying still."

SONNET 144

Sonnet 144 is the only sonnet that explicitly refers to both the Dark Lady and the young man, the poet's "Two loves." Atypically, the poet removes himself from the love triangle and tries to consider the situation with detachment. The humor of the previous sonnet is missing, and the poet's mood is cynical and mocking, in part because uncertainty about the relationship torments him.

Although the sonnet is unique in presenting the poet's attempt to be objective about the two other figures in the relationship, stylistically it is very similar to others in terms of setting up an antithesis between two warring elements, the youth ("comfort") and the woman ("despair"): "The better angel is a man right fair, / The worser spirit a woman, colored ill." Symbolically, the young man and the woman represent two kinds of love battling for supremacy within the poet's own character: selfless adoration and shameful lust, respectively. However, the poet is a mere spectator now. His greatest fear, one that he cannot face, is that the young man secretly acquiesces to the woman's advances: "And whether that my angel be turned fiend / Suspect I may, yet not directly tell." Unfortunately for the poet, what the outcome of this struggle will be is uncertain: "Yet this shall I ne'er know, but live in doubt, / Till my bad angel fire my good one out." Just what the phrase "fire my good one out" means is debatable. One critic suggests that the phrase means "until the woman infects the youth with venereal disease"; others offer the more innocuous meaning "until the youth grows tired of the woman." Ironically, the uncertainty about the fate of the relationship between the young man and the woman is the only certainty the poet has.

SONNET 145

As the sequel to the previous sonnet, Sonnet 145 is a trivial treatment of love. The mistress grants pity on the poet in contrast to previous sonnets, in which she was merciless. Before, her only words to the poet were "I hate," but once she sees how he "languished for her sake," her hatred turns into mercy. Although the imagery of "fiend" and "heaven and hell" continues from Sonnet 144, the tacit meaning of Sonnet 145 is vastly different from the earlier sonnets. The poet creates suspense up until the sonnet's last two words, when he quickly relieves his gloomy expectations by conveying the mistress' phrase "not you": "I hate . . . not you." Melodramatically, these words "saved [the poet's] life."

SONNET 146

The poet now somberly ponders why his soul, as "Lord" of his body, spends so much of its time seeking earthly desires when it should be most concerned about ensuring its immortality. The first eight lines are a series of questions addressed to the soul. Why, the poet asks, when life on earth is so short, does his soul waste itself pining after the woman: "Why so large cost, having so short a lease, / Dost thou upon thy fading mansion spend?" Here the "fading mansion," which is symbolic of the woman and represents the temporal world, contrasts to the immortality promised in the Bible's Psalm 23: "Surely goodness and mercy shall follow me all the days of my life, and I will dwell in the house of the Lord for ever."

In the third quatrain, the poet directs his soul about how best to earn salvation. Learn from the body's experience, he suggests, and let the lesson of the body's being rejected by the woman not be wasted: "Then, soul, live thou upon thy servant's loss, / And let that pine to aggravate thy store." What has before been important and all-consuming—that is, a sexual union—is transient; the soul is not.

The sonnet's piously spiritual reflection is particularly felt in the final couplet, in which the feeding metaphor suggests the image of "Devouring Time." The poet's argument extends the one made in line 12, "Within be fed, without be rich no more." Because death is an inevitable fact of life, the soul needs to prepare itself for when that time comes. Once the soul ensures its immortality, death has no hold, for "there's no more dying then"—the soul becomes eternal.

SONNET 147

The final sonnets concerning the mistress, beginning with this one, return the poet to the disturbed state of previous sonnets. The image of feeding in Sonnet 146 continues in Sonnet 147, only now the feeding is not on death but on illness, and there is no possibility of immortality from lusting after the mistress: "My love is as a fever . . . / . . . / Feeding on that which doth preserve the ill, / Th' uncertain sickly appetite to please." Completely apparent is the poet's inability to separate himself from the relationship.

The poet's reasoning completely fails him. Reason, in the form of a physician, has left him because it can do nothing more to save him from the despair of loving the mistress. Again he acknowledges that his soul's immortality is beyond reach: "Desire is death. . . . / Past cure I am, now reason is past care." His thoughts now move madly, expressed in such terms as "frantic mad," "evermore unrest," "madmen's," and "At random." Despite his ability in the concluding couplet to differentiate between his expectations of his relationship with the woman and the outcome of that relationship, his despondent tone indicates that he is too far gone ever to regain self-confidence.

SONNET 148

In Sonnet 148, a companion to the previous sonnet, the poet admits that his judgment is blind when it comes to love. Again his eyes are false and misperceive reality, and reason has fled him: "O me, what eyes hath Love put in my head, / Which have no correspondence with true sight." Acknowledging the possibility that love metaphorically blinds his judgment, he then attempts to rationalize his predicament. How does the world know that what he sees is false and that what the world considers false is not really true? Although the poet admits his failings, nonetheless he cannot surmount his unhealthy dependency on the woman and his driving passion to rekindle their sexual relationship.

SONNET 149

Sonnet 149 recalls the poet's abject defense of the youth's insulting behavior. The main theme, however, is the conflict between reason and infatuation. Bemoaning the woman's treatment of him even more fervently than before, the poet is quickly slipping into madness: "Canst thou, O cruel, say I love thee not / When I against myself with thee partake?" Such questioning continues throughout the sonnet, with each question designed to convince the woman of all that the poet sacrifices for her benefit. The poet has even gone so far as to forego all friendships with other people. He asks her, "Who hateth thee that I do call my friend? / On whom frown'st thou that I do fawn upon?" Having alienated himself from his friends, the poet now finds himself in the ironic position of having alienated himself from the woman because of his blinding love for her. His calling the woman "love" in the concluding couplet balances his first calling her "O cruel" in line 1: "But, love, hate on, for now I know thy mind; / Those that can see thou lov'st, and I am blind." The woman, then, rejects the poet for the very reason that he is losing his mind—his unreasoning passion for her.

SONNET 150

Using a more rational tone than in the previous sonnet, the poet tries to understand why he cannot completely break from the woman. He shifts his approach, asking what incredible power the woman uses to enslave him; earlier he had asked himself what his own character flaws were that bound him to her. Again written as a series of questions to the woman, the poet asks the woman, "O, from what pow'r hast thou this pow'rful might / With insufficiency my heart to sway?" Contrary to all sense, the poet appeals for pity from his mistress. Her sexual powers have unbalanced his judgment and inflamed his imagination. Promiscuity, the least flattering thing about the woman, is what he loves.

SONNET 151

If the poet ever hoped that his soul would win out over his body, as he does in Sonnet 146, and that his reason would return to govern his senses, he was sadly mistaken. In Sonnet 151, his body's lust for the woman completely controls his actions and thoughts. Resignedly he admits to the woman, "For, thou betraying me, I do betray / My nobler part [his soul] to my gross body's treason." Bawdily, the poet degrades the relationship to an erotic level in which the image of his erect penis is the controlling image of the sonnet: ". . . flesh stays no farther reason, / But, rising at thy name, does point out thee / As his triumphant prize." The phrase "To stand in thy affairs" suggests sexual penetration, and the sonnet ends with yet another image of the poet's erection: "Her 'love' for whose dear love I rise and fall."

SONNET 152

The end of the relationship between the poet and the woman becomes apparent. Addressing the woman with a sense of shame and outrage, the poet is fully conscious of his own adultery and that of his mistress, as well as her infidelity to him and his lack of moral perception: "In loving thee thou know'st I am forsworn, / But thou art twice forsworn." A reconciliation between the poet and the woman is suggested, but subsequently the poet accuses her of "vowing new hate after new love bearing."

Sonnet 152 summarizes much of the poet's past feelings and actions concerning the woman. Self-pityingly he cries, "I am perjured most," and then follows this claim with a litany of how the woman has forsaken all of his oaths to her. In a rare act of perception, he acknowledges just how blind love has made him: "And, to enlighten thee, gave eyes to blindness, / Or made them swear against the thing they see." The concluding couplet emphasizes the irony of the woman's dark appearance, which in previous sonnets the poet characterized as fair, and of her fair character, which he now realizes is metaphorically dark, or immoral: "For I have sworn thee fair: more perjured I, / To swear against the truth so foul a lie!" Some editions read, "more perjured eye," with a pun on "I"; others read, "more perjured I," which echoes the phrase "I am perjured most" from line 6. However, whether the phrase is correctly conveyed with "I" or "eye" is relatively inconsequential: The poet and his "eye" have been inseparable throughout the sonnets, and both are unable to perceive reality using reason rather than passion.

SONNETS 153 AND 154: CUPID

These two sonnets, which may be considered as appendices to the preceding sonnet story, do not touch upon any of the major themes in the sonnets. In Sonnet 153, after Cupid, god of love, falls asleep, a "maid of Dian's" steals Cupid's "love-kindling fire" and extinguishes it in a golden valley's fountain. As the fountain absorbs the heat from the fire, the water acts as a curative potion for "strange maladies"—for example, love sickness. However, the poet finds the best cure for his passion in his mistress' eyes.

Sonnet 154 tells a similar story as the one in Sonnet 153. Cupid falls asleep and a nymph steals his "heart-inflaming brand." She quenches the brand in a cool well, but the poet, who has come to the well to find relief from his love for the mistress, continues to suffer: "Love's fire heats water, water cools not love." The poet's disease is incurable, as we have known it must always be.

- **Dian**   the goddess of chastity, Diana.

- **votary**   nymph of Diana, votaress.

CRITICAL ESSAY

IS SHAKESPEARE SHAKESPEARE?

Many books present facts, reasonable suppositions, traditions, and speculations concerning the life and career of William Shakespeare. Taken as a whole, these materials give a comprehensive picture of England's foremost dramatic poet. Tradition and sober supposition are not necessarily false because they lack proof of their existence. However, readers interested in Shakespeare should distinguish between facts and unfounded beliefs about his life.

From one point of view, modern scholars are fortunate to know as much as they do about a man of middle-class origin who left a small country town and embarked on a professional career in late sixteenth- and early seventeenth-century London. From another point of view, today's scholars know surprisingly little about the writer who has influenced the English language and its drama and poetry for more than three hundred years. Sparse and scattered as the facts of his life are, they are sufficient to prove that a man from Stratford by the name of William Shakespeare wrote the major portion of the thirty-seven plays that scholars attribute to him. Here is a brief look at the known facts of Shakespeare's life:

- Although no one knows the exact date of Shakespeare's birth, he was baptized on Wednesday, April 26, 1564. His father was John Shakespeare, tanner, glover, dealer in grain, and a town official of Stratford; his mother, Mary, was the daughter of Robert Arden, a prosperous gentleman farmer.
- Under a bond dated November 28, 1582, Shakespeare and Anne Hathaway entered into a marriage contract. The baptism of their eldest child, Susanna, took place in May, 1583. One year and nine months later, their twins, Hamnet and Judith (named for the poet's friends, Hamnet and Judith Sadler), were christened.
- Early in 1596, Shakespeare, in his father's name, applied to the College of Heralds for a coat of arms. In 1599, Shakespeare applied for the right to combine (quarter) his coat of arms with that of his mother.

- In May 1597, Shakespeare purchased New Place, the finest residential property in Stratford at that time, indicating that he must have achieved success for himself by then.
- In July 1605, Shakespeare purchased half the annual tithes, or taxes, on certain agricultural products from parcels of land, receiving income from his investment, and almost doubling his capital.
- In 1612, Shakespeare's testimony was recorded in a court dispute between Christopher Mountjoy, in whose household Shakespeare had roomed, and Mountjoy's son-in-law.
- Shakespeare was left five pounds in the will of John Combe, a friend and fellow resident of Stratford, who died on July 12, 1614.

On March 25, 1616, William Shakespeare revised his last will and testament. He died on April 23 of the same year, and his body was buried in the Stratford church.

These records and similar ones prove the existence of William Shakespeare in Stratford and in London during this period.

Similarly, the evidence establishing William Shakespeare as the foremost playwright of his day is positive and persuasive:

- Robert Greene's *Greenes groats-worth of witte, bought with a million of repentance*, in which he attacked Shakespeare, a *mere* actor, for presuming to write plays in competition with Greene and his fellow playwrights, was entered in the *Stationers' Register* on September 20, 1592.
- In 1594, Shakespeare acted before Queen Elizabeth, and in 1594–95, his name appeared as one of the shareholders of the Lord Chamberlain's Company, a famous acting troupe.
- Francis Meres, in his *Palladis Tamia* (1598), called Shakespeare "mellifluous and hony-tongued" and compared the excellence of his plays with those of Plautus and Seneca.
- Shakespeare's name appears as one of the owners of the open-air Globe Theatre in 1599.
- On May 19, 1603, he and his fellow actors received a patent from James I designating them as King's Men.
- Late in 1608 or early in 1609, Shakespeare and his colleagues purchased the indoor Blackfriars Theatre and began using it as their winter location.

One of the most impressive of all proofs of Shakespeare's authorship of his plays is the *First Folio* of 1623, with the dedicatory verse that appears in it. John Heminge and Henry Condell, members of Shakespeare's own acting company, stated that they collected and issued the plays as a memorial to their fellow actor.

Certainly the most diligent of scholars does not know and cannot explain many things about Shakespeare's genius and career. However, the facts that do exist are sufficient to establish Shakespeare's identity as a man and as the author of the thirty-seven plays and the poems and sonnets that reputable critics acknowledge to be his.

REVIEW QUESTIONS AND ESSAY TOPICS

(1) Select two sonnets from each of the two major divisions (Sonnets 1–126 and 127–154). How do they differ in mood and the treatment of love?

(2) Which sonnets do you find most shocking, and why?

(3) In the sonnets, what views does Shakespeare express regarding the nature of true love and the miseries of misguided love?

(4) Write an essay in which you discuss the poet's changing attitudes toward the young man.

(5) How does the poet's love for the young man differ from his love for the Dark Lady?

(6) How does Shakespeare indicate that time may be conquered? How do the sonnets themselves indicate that time may be conquered?

(7) Discuss the them of immortality as presented in the sonnets, citing specific lines as support for your views.

(8) What role does nature play in the sonnets? Is nature linked with one specific theme? If so, which theme, and how?

SELECTED BIBLIOGRAPHY

Books and Articles

BLOOM, HAROLD, ed. *Shakespeare's Sonnets and Poems*. Broomall, PA. Chelsea House Publishers, 1999.

BURKE, KATE. "From Page to Page: The Use of Shakespeare's Sonnets in Introducing Intimidated Students to His Drama." *Iowa State Journal of Research* 62.3 (February 1988): 347–58.

DE GRAZIA, MARGRETA. "The Scandal of Shakespeare's Sonnets." *Shakespeare Survey* 46 (1993): 35–49.

DUBROW, HEATHER. "'Incertainties Now Crown Themselves Assur'd': The Politics of Plotting Shakespeare's Sonnets." *Shakespeare Quarterly* 47.3 (Fall 1996): 291–305.

DUNCAN-JONES, KATHERINE. "What Are Shakespeare's Sonnets Called?" *Essays in Criticism* 47.1 (January 1997): 1–12.

HEDLEY, JANE. "Since First Your Eye I Eyed: Shakespeare's Sonnets and the Poetics of Narcissism." *Style* 28.1 (Spring 1994): 1–30.

MISCHO, JOHN B. "'That Use is not Forbidden Usury': Shakespeare's Procreation Sonnets and the Problem of Usury." *Subjects on the World's Stage: Essays on British Literature of the Middle Ages and the Renaissance*. Eds. David C. Allen and Robert A. White. Newark: University of Delaware Press, 1995. 262–79.

PEQUINGEY, JOSEPH. *Such Is My Love: A Study of Shakespeare's Sonnets*. Chicago: University of Chicago Press, 1985.

ROBERTS, JOSEPHINE A. "'Thou Maist Have Thy Will': The Sonnets of Shakespeare and His Stepsisters." *Shakespeare Quarterly* 47.4 (Winter 1996): 407–23.

VENDLER, HELEN. *The Art of Shakespeare's Sonnets*. Cambridge, MA: Harvard University Press, 1997.

Online Resources

"Mr. William Shakespeare and the Internet." www.daphne.palomar.edu/shakespeare

"Shakespeare 101: A Student Guide." www.ulen.com/shakespeare/students

"Shakespeare and the Globe Theatre." www.rdg.ac.uk/globe

"Shakespeare on the Internet." www.engl.uvic.ca/shakespeare/Faculty/MBHomePage/ShakSites1

"Shakespeare Web." www.shakespeare.com

"4Shakespeare.com." http://4Shakespeare/4Anything.com